Kate
KRAY

ULTIMATE HARD MEN

The Truth About the Toughest Men in the World

First published in the UK by John Blake Publishing
an imprint of Bonnier Books UK
4th Floor, Victoria House
Bloomsbury Square,
London, WC1B 4DA
England

Owned by Bonnier Books
Sveavägen 56, Stockholm, Sweden

www.facebook.com/johnblakebooks

twitter.com/jblakebooks

First published in paperback in 2005, this edition published in 2022

Paperback: 978-1-78946-270-8
Ebook: 978-1-78219-156-8
Audio: 978-1-78946-323-1

Design by www.envydesign.co.uk

Printed and bound in Great Britain by Clays Ltd, Elcograf S.p.A

1 3 5 7 9 10 8 6 4 2

John Blake Publishing is an imprint of Bonnier Books UK
www.bonnierbooks.co.uk

ULTIMATE HARD MEN

Contents

Prologue

The men you are about to meet in these pages are hardcore.
A hard core of hard men.

There are three key ingredients that make a hard man, and
all tough guys have these three things in common: the three
Rs – Respect, Reputation and can have a 'Row'.

DICTIONARY DEFINITIONS:

Respect – An attitude of deference, admiration, regard,
the state of being honoured.

Reputation – A high opinion generally held about a
person.

Row – A person who fights and has determination.
A battle, struggle, physical combat or punch-up.

The three Rs were the only criteria needed to be included in this book. I interviewed hundreds of men. Some made the grade and some didn't – some I liked and some I didn't. But whether I liked them or not wasn't important. Whether they liked each other or not wasn't important either. The only thing that mattered was that aggression was paramount and part and parcel of their everyday life. They eat it, sleep it and breathe it. Violence is their life. This book includes murder, armed robbery and lots of gratuitous violence. I'm not glorifying it or trying to justify the violence, I'm just trying to understand the reasons why some men are prepared to go all the way. If we can understand them perhaps we don't have to fear them.

Everyone in this book is extraordinary in their own way and they all have a tale or two. Some of the things they say are horrifying. They don't try to make excuses for their actions or justify what they've done. It's said and done, and that's it! They are from right across the board: SAS, murderers, gangsters, terrorists, strongmen and street-fighters – you name it, they're all included. I've interviewed hundreds of men and you quickly get to grips with who matters and who doesn't, who has respect and reputation and who hasn't.

Most of these men are aggressive in one way or another, many violent. Some will cut you and laugh while you're bleeding. All inhabit a world, a kind of parallel world, which ordinary people would find totally alien – they catch glimpses of it only occasionally on TV. But that's sugar-coated. It's not the real thing. This is.

My only rule was that if the tough guy was a bully, there was no way they'd be in my book – full-stop. If they were loud, brash or giving it the 'big 'un' – 'I'm gonna do this and I'm gonna do that', then I left them out. Every man in this book has said, 'I'm not a hard man, I'm not a tough guy, I'm not 'orrible – I'm a nice bloke.' I found that more chilling than a man trying to convince me that he's this and he's that.

One man who needs hardly any introduction is Roy 'Pretty Boy' Shaw. He's a man among men. A homme de substance – a man of substance. He's a boxer, a fighter, a walking, talking mean machine. Roy is a self-confessed ruthless bastard and if you're unfortunate enough to have Roy come after you, beware, because Hell comes with him!

Take Johnny Adair or 'Mad Dog' – the political animal, a man alleged to have killed thirty or forty people. He didn't need to convince me that he was a force to be reckoned with, he just is. I could sense the danger oozing from every pore in his body. I could feel it, almost taste it.

While interviewing Johnny Adair, I can honestly say that anything could have happened. A hired hitman could have had him in his sights or a strategically placed bomb could have had Johnny's name on it. Who knows? There have been ten attempts to kill him and he's only thirty-seven. Maybe Lady Luck is looking down on Johnny Adair, or he's got a guardian angel, or perhaps he's too much of a handful for just one man, because if you attack Johnny Adair you'd better hope and pray that you kill him, because if you don't, you'll be the one pushing up daisies.

Big John Daniels. The sheer size of the man, the way he holds himself, his very demeanour is enough to intimidate most people. Everything about him spells violence. His dark shades shield his black crushed-velvet eyes that stare into a secret, hostile world into which no one dares enter. He was the only man hard enough to be entrusted with guarding Ronnie Kray's body before the funeral.

Errol Francis is the World Kick-Boxing champion and Steven Spielberg's minder. He works with all the stars in Britain and America, not only as their bodyguard but also as their personal trainer. He mixes and mingles in the highest of circles. He's a whopping mountain of a man – touch him and he feels like rock. But Errol has got his feet firmly on the ground. When you meet him, he makes you feel like you're special. He smiles all the time and his laugh is infectious.

Then there's Carlton Leach, football hooligan, member of the notorious Inter City Firm (ICF) and now minder, whose closest friend was blasted to death with a shotgun.

Charlie Seiga, from Liverpool, whom the police codenamed Killer.

Gangsters like the late Tony Lambrianou, who stood with Ronnie in the dock.

Danny Reece, an armed robber, who is married to Linda Calvey, the woman they call the Black Widow after the spider who kills her mate after sex. Both Danny and Linda are now serving life for murder.

PROLOGUE

There are heroes here – and, of course, villains.

After talking to so many of them, I can't help but notice how, despite the fact they are all so very different, they have so much in common.

These are all hard men. Those on the right side of the law seem to have done OK for themselves and some are, I'm sure, destined for fame.

Those who have, shall we say, strayed across the line haven't always been so lucky.

Many of these men have had really difficult childhoods. Many learnt to fight when they were young because they had to – from very early on, the name of the game was survival. Many witnessed violence, either within their family or around them, when they were youngsters. The education they received was poor and some of them didn't stand much of a chance. Most turned to crime to get money, pure and simple.

Many of the men included in the book dislike each other with a passion. One man, whose name I won't mention, shoved a gun up a rival's nose. That rival is also included in the book. After seeing his photograph, the man I was interviewing decided to pull out. I explained to him that he didn't have to like the man or associate himself with him in any way, shape or form. The fact of the matter is that they are both hard men and I wanted them both in the book. He is not a fool and rose above his hatred. He shrugged, 'Yeah, fuck him!'

After that I quickly learnt to be diplomatic, and careful who I told was included. Each man would sneer and say the same thing: 'I'd do 'im any day – he's not a hard man.' So I decided not to show any of them the photographs or tell them who was in the book. Not because I was bothered about upsetting them, but because I didn't want them to pull out.

Ronnie Kray had a little black address book full to bursting with telephone numbers of conmen, murderers and tough guys from all over the country. After we married, I kept a copy of the book in case it was lost or stolen in Broadmoor. I automatically assumed that everybody in the book knew each other, but they didn't; they all knew Ron, though. He was the kingpin in the middle – the 'Colonel'.

Occasionally I had to phone these men for various 'bits of work'. They were villains from as far afield as Wales, Scotland, Ireland and the USA. I got to know them all. Some of them were crazy and unhinged, but they became my friends and, from them, I made more friends. Now I've got a Thomson Local directory – the Who's Who in the criminal fraternity!

The more I got to know these men, the more they intrigued me.

I started asking them questions – but not about how many people they'd killed or whose body had been buried in which motorway foundations. I wanted to know what made a hard man. What makes a man dangerous? Size? Love? Money? Passion? Loyalty? Or was it all of these things rolled into one? Is there a link between them? Are there similarities? What makes a man kill? What makes him different? What drives a man to go all the way? Is it in his background? Was he bullied as a child? Is it situation or circumstance? I wanted to interview men who have fire in their bellies and passion in their souls. Those who've got something going on beneath their tough exterior. I wanted to know what makes them tick. Do they have to learn to kill or does it come naturally? The questions were endless.

Not all the men I interviewed are from the underworld; there are also law-abiding, straight-up tough guys. Some of the men found it difficult talking about themselves. Some were shy and awkward. But after a couple of visits, they relaxed and started to open up. They'd protected themselves for so long and never let anyone close enough to see them vulnerable or exposed.

Although they were tough men on the street – they can have a row, and can kill – the one thing they were really nervous about was being interviewed and the thing they hated most was the tape recorder. Then it dawned on me that when someone is nicked, the first thing the Old Bill say is, 'You do not have to say anything. But, it may harm your defence if you do not mention when questioned something which you later rely on in court. Anything you do say may be given in evidence.' Every single one of the men was suspicious of the tape recorder. They kept looking at it. It made them uncomfortable and they became 'legal' experts, as if defending themselves. Their voices changed and they started trying to talk in a 'solicitor'-type voice: 'Oh no, I proceeded down the road in an orderly fashion. Those nasty handcuffs were chafing me!' At that point I'd stop the interview, turn the tape recorder off and just get them to relax for a bit.

What's missing from this book, because words don't do them justice, were the men's many gestures. On numerous occasions during our conversations, they'd leap up from their seats and demonstrate with clenched fists exactly how they'd whacked someone, or emphasise the venomous thrust when stabbing a victim. But they never did it to brag or show off; it was simply so that I could get it exactly right. It was then that I saw these men come alive – when they re-enacted their many murderous attacks.

The question I'm asked continually – and usually it's more of an accusation than a question – is: 'Aren't you glamorising crime by writing about these people, by giving them airtime?'

The answer to that is: 'No, I'm not.'

No, no, no!

I don't write my books in a tongue-in-cheek way. I am fully aware that many of the things these men have done is unacceptable.

Films like *Snatch* and *Lock, Stock* ... do much more to glamorise crime than I do. Those films are definitely tongue-in-cheek – they describe horrific crimes but put a joke or two in so that makes it OK. And everyone thinks it's OK. I tell it how it is, how it really is. I don't sugar-coat it. Because this isn't a glamorous world to be in. I think that often it's an extremely unpleasant world to be in. But people have always been fascinated by it, since the days of Robin Hood or Dick Turpin, and they always will be.

This is how it is.

So many of the men I have met have ended up spending the best part of their lives in prison – what a waste! As a result many of them have lost their wives, their children, their homes. They end up with virtually nothing ... and no one.

I can count on the fingers of one hand how many people in this world have come out with a fortune – most haven't got anything but diddly-squat.

I don't glamorise crime. Ron and Reg were big-time but, in the end, even if you are big-time, one of three things is going to happen to you – either you will go to prison for a very, very long time, and like Ron, you'll end up dying in prison; or, like Reg, they'll let you out just in time to die.

Or you'll end up being popped in a country lane.

I know many people in this parallel world and some of them are in their sixties, even their seventies, and they're still 'at it'. They still need the money. They're always looking for The Big One, the one that will set them up for life so they don't have to do it any more. That's the problem.

I like to call them the 'weekend millionaires'. You can always tell if they've been up to something because, come the weekend, they've got the Rolexes on, they've got the Armani suits on, they're being Charlie Big Bollocks in the pubs, buying everyone a drink.

But if they can't keep up that lifestyle, they have to go on to do another blag, or whatever it is they do. In fact, far from being glamorous, it's a very stressful world to live in. I think through writing these books and interviewing all these people, the thing that comes out of it most is that there's really nothing like a straight pound note.

So no, I don't think I am glamorising them. Those who have stumbled on to the wrong side of the law, well, not one of them says it's a good world to be in because it's not.

But this is the truth. This isn't *Lock, Stock and Smoking Bollocks*. This is real. I tell it how it is. I tell it from the hip. And these men have been included in this book because they're going to tell you how it is.

There were two questions that came up time and time again while I was writing *Ultimate Hard Men*. Everybody I spoke to wanted to know which one was the toughest and why? I know who's the toughest. I hope you can read between the lines and draw your own conclusion as to who is the ultimate hard man in Great Britain.

Roy Shaw

Roy Shaw wears designer gear, has a cool million in the bank, a beautiful home and a shiny red Bentley Corniche. He hasn't gotten where he is today by being a nice guy. He got there by being the toughest. Everything about Roy spells violence. He is fifteen stone of squat, solid muscle, which knots and pops under his silk shirt when he moves. His small, piercing-blue eyes are set above a corrugated nose. Roy appears to stare with an unnerving intensity into a secret world of hostility and hatred. In short, he is a walking, talking killing machine.

I met Roy Shaw eleven years ago and in 1999 I was the co-writer of his book, *Pretty Boy*. I've got to say that Roy is probably the finest man I have ever met and I've met them all – yardies, gangsters and hard men from all over the country. Indeed, I was married to the most infamous gangster in British history – Ronnie Kray. Ron was the only man who I could truthfully say had the

1

look of the Devil in his eyes when he was angry. I didn't think I'd ever see that look again until I met Roy Shaw. Some would say he is Lucifer, Beelzebub, the Prince of Darkness.

But he hasn't got horns sticking out from the top of his head or cloven hooves and a tail; he's just a man, and one with strict principles and morals. Roy has laid down his own boundaries for himself and has never overstepped the invisible mark or, more importantly, allowed anyone else to.

Trust is a very hard thing to come by these days, but I would, undoubtedly, trust Roy Shaw with my life. If you are lucky enough to make a friend of Roy, then he is a bloody good friend. Make an enemy of him and beware, because he's a typical male – made up of frogs and snails and puppy dogs' tails. When he's good, he's very, very good and when he's bad, he's horrid.

BACKGROUND

I was born in Stepney, east London, within the sound of the Bow Bells. I'm a true Cockney, a Londoner through and through. I was a street urchin, a ragamuffin. I grew up in the war years when times were hard. Our family didn't have much in the way of money, but we had plenty of love.

At the tender age of ten I discovered the gift that God had given me – the power of punch. From then on, I became a rascal, getting myself into all sorts of trouble.

I was a man on a mission with nothing to lose and a lot to prove.

I became a professional boxer, training under the guidance of Mickey Duff. I had ten professional fights with ten wins, six of them knock-outs.

LIFE OF CRIME

I've been in and out of prison nearly all my life for various different reasons; a little bit of this, a little bit that – comme ci, comme ça – but mainly for crimes of violence. I've spent approximately twenty-four years behind bars.

WEAPONRY

I'd use my fists, but if someone was armed then I'd also be armed and I'd kill them.

TOUGHEST MOMENT

I was ten years old. I was lying in bed when I heard Mum scream. My elder sisters looked after me while Mum went to the hospital. When she came back, her face was ashen. She sat me down on the sofa, her eyes red and puffy.

'Daddy's dead,' she whispered.

There had been a terrible accident. A lorry had swerved out of control and one of the pedals of my father's motorbike hit the kerb. Dad tried to regain control of his bike, but it was no good; he hit a lamp-post head-on and was killed instantly. That was a long time ago, but I remember it as if it was yesterday and I'm not ashamed to say that it still brings a tear to my eye.

IS THERE ANYONE YOU ADMIRE?
No.

DO YOU BELIEVE IN CAPITAL PUNISHMENT?
Yes, I most definitely do, for paedophiles, rapists and perverts.

A man that commits crimes against women and children is not a man, he's a fucking dog and deserves to die like one.

IS PRISON A DETERRENT?
No. I was a hard-working kid before I was put away, then I got to know all the 'toughies'. Going off the straight and narrow is nothing new – it's a well-trod path, a natural progression. Borstal, prison, then Broadmoor. I wasn't the first to be put away and I certainly won't be the last, just the handsomest!

WHAT WOULD HAVE DETERRED YOU FROM A LIFE OF CRIME?
Nothing.

WHAT MAKES A TOUGH GUY?
When a child is born it has no concept of skin colour, religion or prejudice. It has to learn how to walk, talk, hate and fight. I think you've got to learn how to be a

tough guy. It took a long time and lots of hard graft for me to become as nasty as I am.

ROY'S FINAL THOUGHT

In 1999, I wrote my autobiography, *Pretty Boy*. It was at number one in the bestsellers list for more than eight weeks and there is talk of my life story being made into a feature film. I'm not embarrassed to say that I'm as proud as punch, if not a little surprised.

Since writing my book, I've had literally hundreds of letters from kids all over the country, some from as far away as Australia, saying that my story has given them hope and inspiration. That's the best compliment I've ever received. If I can help prevent one youngster from being bullied, then writing the book was well worth the effort. As a young boy I was bullied; it affected me badly.

My father died when I was ten years old. After that sad day, something inside me died – I just snapped. I wouldn't allow the bullies to bash me any more. Almost overnight I turned from a meek, mild boy into, some would say, a ruthless bastard. If I'm truthful, I'd agree and say that, yes, I am a ruthless man. But I didn't set out to get a reputation, that was never my intention. It just happened.

I've hurt, killed and done some wicked acts of violence throughout my life, but only if a man deserved it. I can honestly put my hand on my heart and say that I have never hurt any women or children. So, I have no regrets or the need to unburden myself and ask anyone for forgiveness. If I hurt ya – fuck ya – you deserved it.

I don't live in the past, because if you live in the past you die a bit each day. I have no pity or conscience and have been called the Devil; maybe I am, but when I die, I know that God will shake my hand and welcome me into Heaven with open arms because, basically, I'm a nice, ruthless bastard.

Johnny Adair

I'd heard about Johnny through the prison grapevine. Often, his name would crop up in conversation, but I'd never actually met him. In September 1999, I saw a small article in the _Sun_. There was a photograph of Johnny Adair being released from the Maze prison under the Good Friday Peace Treaty. He was the 293rd prisoner to be released and, as he walked, or should I say strutted, from the Maze, he looked every bit as dangerous as I'd heard he was.

I decided to include Johnny in _Ultimate Hard Men_ because he fitted the criteria: he demands respect and has a fearsome reputation, but mainly he can have a 'row'.

It's one thing to decide to put someone in a book, but then I've got to find them and convince them to take part.

I certainly didn't want to put word out on the street that I was looking for Johnny or, indeed, that anyone was looking for him. I know from experience that dangerous men are extremely paranoid.

Usually, if I want to contact a villain I make a call or two and I'll have the number in my hand within hours, but Northern Ireland is not my manor. However, it was amazingly simple to find Johnny Adair. I rang Directory Enquiries and asked for numbers of political parties in Belfast. The operator gave me five or six different organisations and I started to make my calls. I explained each time that I was a journalist and wanted to speak to a man called Johnny Adair.

Instinctively, I felt that what I was doing was not 'politically correct', but I needed to find Johnny. There was a wall of silence. Every answer was the same, a curt, 'You won't find him here. You won't find him there.'

Then I struck lucky. A lady I spoke to shiftily gave me a number and then hung up. I telephoned the number and asked to speak to Johnny Adair. A man with a strong, gruff Irish accent answered, 'What do you want him for?'

I explained who I was and that I was writing a book. The voice on the line became softer, no longer hostile.

He introduced himself as Matt Kincade and said that he had read a couple of my books while serving time in the Maze and that Johnny Adair was a friend of his.

The whole exercise had been like looking for a needle in a haystack, and hopefully, I'd found it! Within days, Johnny was in touch, but was reluctant to commit to any firm meeting. It was all very cloak and dagger. I told him I would travel to Ireland on 11 November. He gave me a telephone number and told me to ring it when I arrived. With that tiny snippet of information, I booked my ticket on the early-morning flight from Luton to Belfast.

My easyJet flight to Northern Ireland was delayed – damn, I didn't want to be late! I was going to meet Johnny Adair, or 'Mad Dog' as he is known. I sat on the plane waiting for take-off. I was fed-up; it was the one interview I didn't want to miss.

My friends and family had warned me not to go. They all said the same; that I was getting in too deep. I'd heard wild stories about Johnny Adair kidnapping Catholics and chopping them up. Each story was more bizarre than the last. I didn't take any notice; to me it was all just hearsay.

Then I heard it from a good, reliable source that I really shouldn't go; it was too dangerous and I was getting out of my depth.

Being the flippant fool that I am, I just replied that I wasn't Catholic or Protestant, but in actual fact I was Salvation Army. I was a Sunbeam so, as far as I was concerned, I was quite safe – or as safe as I could be.

We landed in Belfast on a cold, grey November morning. I made my way to the Stormont Hotel by cab. I was now apprehensive, unsure what I was walking into. Maybe everyone had been right after all, and I was putting my life in danger needlessly. My minder stayed close to me the whole time and the photographer said nothing through fear.

When we reached the hotel, we ordered coffee in the lounge area and I rummaged in my briefcase for the small scrap of paper with the telephone number that Johnny Adair had given me. My instructions were to wait; Johnny would ring my mobile phone at 10.00 a.m. sharp. On the button, my phone rang – it was Johnny.

From the start, he was paranoid. He thought it was a set-up and said that if I wanted to speak to him then I was to go to the Shankhill Road.

I said no; I was a girl, I'd come to his backyard and it was only right that he came to the Stormont to see me. He laughed. 'I'll be there in half an hour.'

I waited outside the hotel for Johnny to arrive. I'm used to dealing with paranoid men and I wanted to put Johnny at ease and, more than anything, show him that it wasn't a set-up and his life wasn't in any danger. I told the photographer to wait inside and my minder to stay close.

Half an hour later I noticed a car circle the hotel. I watched it drive round once, and then again, before pulling up in front of me. Driving the car was a huge man. Sitting next to him was Johnny Adair. He climbed from the car, eyes scanning everywhere. His minder did the same, hand inside his jacket. Johnny walked towards me, his greeting warm and sincere. I introduced him to my minder, and he introduced me to his. Johnny's accent was so deep that I had difficulty understanding him.

'This is Winker,' he said, pointing to his minder.

'Sorry?' I replied, with a puzzled look.

'Winker ... this is Winker.'

I shook his minder's hand and said, 'Nice to meet you, Wanker!'

For a moment there was a deathly silence. My minder looked away in horror. Winker's face could have curdled milk. Johnny Adair roared with laughter and, from that moment on, the ice was broken.

To start, the Irishman wanted to do the interview in the back of a car while it drove round the streets of Belfast, but I convinced Johnny to go inside the hotel.

As we walked through the car park, a police car drove past. Johnny stopped dead in his tracks and glared at the patrol car. The officers inside looked at Johnny. I saw the panic in their eyes. Johnny stared daggers at them. They looked away. Johnny shot a glance at his minder and they both smiled.

We settled in the hotel foyer and ordered our coffees. I sat with Johnny on a sofa while our minders and the photographer sat some distance away.

Before he agreed to be in the book, Johnny wanted to know what it was all about. I explained about the book and showed him some of the photos of a couple of men who were already included. In a strong Ian Paisley accent he said, 'I'm not a gangster. I'm not a fighter. I'm a soldier of war – a fucking terrorist!'

The entire time I was in Johnny's company I felt that at any moment something could happen. I didn't quite know what, but it was extremely dangerous being in his

11

presence. His eyes flickered round the room all the time, scanning and surveying, watching everybody's move – as did his bodyguard.

We started to talk and he became a little more relaxed until somebody sat behind me. His piercing-blue eyes widened with alarm. He motioned to Winker. Suddenly they were on alert.

'Do you know the man sitting behind you?' he whispered.

I glanced over my shoulder and shook my head. It was obvious that Johnny was now uncomfortable. He never took his eyes off the man and Winker stayed close. He may have thought the man was from the security forces, the IRA, or just a hitman who'd come to kill him.

It all seemed a little far-fetched until Johnny took his hat off and showed me the hole in the back of his head, the size of a fifty-pence piece. Two months earlier, he'd been shot in the back of the head at a UB40 concert.

Then he lifted his sweater and showed me a hole in his side and one in his leg. He had been almost cut in half in another attack. In total, there had been over ten attempts to kill him.

As Johnny talked and his story slowly unravelled, it became clear it was a tale not about money, or a grudge – Johnny Adair was fighting for what he truly believed in, which was for peace in Northern Ireland. I told him it was difficult for me to understand, because all we are used to seeing on the mainland are the atrocities that are committed in Ireland.

Before going to Northern Ireland, I didn't have any preconceived ideas about Johnny Adair. But I didn't expect him to be as 'normal', or as warm and friendly as he was. Everyone expects terrorists to be gun-toting thugs, but that's not the case. Johnny spoke with great intellect. There was no malice or bitterness in his voice. It was the cool, controlled way in which he spoke that made him so utterly terrifying. He was normal – just like you and me. Before I went to Northern Ireland I really hadn't known what to expect, but I wasn't prepared for the Johnny Adair that I met.

At the end of the interview Johnny agreed to have a photograph taken outside Stormont Castle, where the peace talks were taking place. We left the hotel and stood on the kerb, waiting to cross the busy main road. There were four lanes full of traffic. Every car in the four lanes stopped to let Johnny cross because they recognised him. It was unbelievable. This is the power he has in Ireland.

Johnny was very amicable until the photographer asked him to turn his head and look at the castle. He refused; Johnny clearly still wasn't sure if it was a set-up. After the photoshoot, he was whisked away by his minder as quickly as he'd arrived.

BACKGROUND

I was born in the Shankhill Road area of Belfast, Northern Ireland. I'm the youngest of five brothers and one sister. As a teenager, I ran with a gang of Protestants. We'd roam the city centre searching for Catholics to hurt, for no other reason than their religion.

To people on the mainland this may sound extreme, but unless you live in Northern Ireland the Troubles are difficult to understand. I can only describe Belfast as two nations – Protestant and Catholic – and, believe me, the two don't mix. It can be likened to the combination of nitroglycerine and a detonator – separately, they are safe, but put them together and it's dynamite! The wars were bloody and there were many casualties on both sides. I bear many scars and war wounds from endless street battles. I think my reputation came from being a paramilitary leader, even before I was involved in the politics of it.

I was a young Loyalist, full of hate and anger, and saw Catholics as my enemy. I was a product of the Troubles; I grew up on the streets. Fighting Catholics was all I knew. I was a loose cannon until I joined the paramilitaries, which gave me the direction I needed. It was then I realised why I was fighting: for peace in my country. Freedom is a passion I truly believe in.

It's every human being's fundamental right to be free and I'd fight until the last breath in my body to achieve this independence. I became ruthless in my quest and would stop at nothing. It was then I earned respect and got my reputation.

LIFE OF CRIME

I've been in and out of jail all my life, all for terrorist offences. In 1995, I was charged with 'Directive Terrorism' and was sentenced to sixteen years. Directive Terrorism covers a lot of things but I can't, for legal and security reasons, talk specifically about what I have done. In September 1999, I was the 293rd prisoner to be released early under the Good Friday peace deal.

WEAPONRY

Again, for legal and security reasons I cannot say what I specialise in.

TOUGHEST MOMENT

I've had many tough moments. There have been ten attempts on my life. I've been attacked with crowbars and hammers and stabbed twice, in the back and in the leg. I've been shot and wounded three times, once by the IRA. They ambushed my car and opened fire with an assault rifle. I was hit in the side of my body. But the worst pain I've ever experienced in my life was being shot at close range in the back of the head. It was the most petrifying moment I've ever had.

It was autumn 1999 and I'd just been released from Ulster's top-security Maze prison on parole. I'd promised to take my wife to a UB40 concert. We'd been looking forward to our first night out in many years. The kids were safely tucked up in bed and the babysitter was due at any time. As we were getting ready, there was nothing to suggest that this night was ever going to be anything out of the ordinary.

The atmosphere at the concert was electrifying; UB40's rhythm contagious. My wife and I swayed to the dulcet tones, 'Red, red wine…' It was good to feel normal again, if only for a moment.

BANG! The panic, the fear, the confusion. My wife screamed. I slumped to the floor with a bullet lodged in the back of my head.

IS THERE ANYONE YOU ADMIRE?

There are people I admire in Ireland who, in my eyes, are heroes. For instance, Michael Stone, the lone sniper in a Catholic graveyard. It's difficult for me to explain and I certainly don't mean any disrespect to London gangsters, but there are things terrorists would do in two days that gangsters wouldn't do in their lifetime. That's just a symptom of what's happening in Northern Ireland. Atrocities aren't being committed on a personal level, it's aimed at the enemy and we believe the things we are doing are part of defending our people. If this means going to the extreme, then so be it.

DO YOU BELIEVE IN CAPITAL PUNISHMENT?

No.

IS PRISON A DETERRENT?

In Ireland, prison is not thought of as a deterrent, although a few years ago things were different and prison would have been harder, but not these days. In Ireland, the paramilitary run the prisons, not the screws. We're not criminals, we're paramilitaries; we're classed as soldiers. When we go to jail, we don't do what they tell us – they do what we tell them.

Jail is not a deterrent, jail is an education. I learnt more about life when I was in jail than I did in the whole of my lifetime when I was out.

In jail, you're confined twenty-four hours a day and that time is spent alone. Outside time just passes you by and you never have time to stop and think about anything. Inside, you're on your own, you analyse everything, you have all the time in the world to think, so it's an education because everything goes through your head about what happened in the past and what might happen in the future. You analyse it all and educate yourself – it's self-education. The fact that you're in jail can be used to your advantage – if you want exams, you learn; if you're into training, you use your time in the gym. That's what I did. I went into jail out of shape and came out in the best shape of my life.

No, jail is not a deterrent, it's an education. The only thing it does is take away your freedom.

WHAT WOULD HAVE DETERRED YOU FROM A LIFE OF CRIME?

Nothing would have deterred me because I fight for what I believe in, and when you believe in something, you follow your heart.

I strongly believe what I've done is right, so I have followed my heart. The only thing that will stop me from fighting is peace in my country.

WHAT MAKES A TOUGH GUY?

Only one man in a thousand is really tough. It's natural – just in them. It's not something you can share or explain; it's just in you and people notice it and feel it.

JOHNNY'S FINAL THOUGHT

I have no regrets in my life except that so many people have lost their lives. It's just a shame that peace didn't happen in Northern Ireland thirty years ago. The peace that we have now and the talks that are presently taking place should have happened in 1969. Then there wouldn't be over three thousand people dead today, both Protestant and Catholic. That's the only regret I have in the role that I played.

In September 1999, I was released from the Maze. I'd served five years of a sixteen-year sentence. Now I'm mellowing back into the community. Things have changed since I've been away – for the better. At last there is peace, but not for me.

When I was inside, I let my guard down. When I came out of prison, I thought I was safe to go to a UB40 concert with my wife – I was wrong.

Now I don't go anywhere without a minder. I have to live in a house that is protected like a fortress; all steel doors and security cameras. I have men sitting at the bottom of my street day and night to watch me and my family. Every day I wake up expecting something to happen and not knowing if it's going to be my last day on earth.

The only thing that gave me a wee bit of breathing space was the shared government, but look what happened to that.

I don't fear for myself, I fear for my family. I believe that it's me with the death sentence hanging over my head. If I thought any different, I would have been up and away years ago.

First and foremost, I have no fear of the IRA or anyone else. If I did, I would be living in England. But I'm not, I'm still living in Belfast. I live fifty yards from a peace line that proves I have no fear of them.

The security forces nicknamed me Johnny 'Mad Dog' Adair. In their eyes, I'd killed over forty people. They built up this myth that I was a Mad Dog who would kill anyone. People expect me to be a fanatical, violent, rabid dog. It's not the case – I'm just Johnny and, deep down inside, I'm a good guy. But, do me a wrong and I'll bring it to your own backyard. You'll go to bed at night and barricade your front door in case Johnny 'Mad Dog' Adair comes looking for you.

Vic Dark

'I played for high stakes and lost. The judge sentenced me to forty-eight years in prison. Standing in the dock were the "cozzers"; they smiled and shook hands, the no-good slags! Next morning, I woke up in one of Her Majesty's Prisons and there I stayed, in a world full of terrorists, crazies and murderers. There is precious little left to truly shock the bejesus out of me, except betrayal by a friend – or a so-called friend!'

I was sitting in a flash office in Tottenham, east London, interviewing Vic Dark – some call him 'The Man'. The office looked like it belonged to JR Ewing from the popular soap *Dallas* – all heavy oak panels and comfortable leather chairs. It was Vic's brother's office, the owner of a successful company. A condition of Vic's parole is that he has a job, so his brother employed him.

'It pissed the screws off when, on my release from

21

prison, my brother picked me up in his brand-spanking-new Bentley convertible,' Vic sniggered.

His mood soon changes when he mentions a former friend, who I'll call 'Jock'. He curses and snarls with anger at having already spent twelve years inside for him. Vic continues, 'I should have shot the slag. Put one in his nut...'

He spoke with such venom and anger, as if it all happened yesterday; the wounds were so obviously still raw. It is a story beyond belief.

He and 'Jock' were on an armed robbery. There was a bit of a hiccup and Vic shot a security guard. To be precise, he blew his fucking thumb off! Some hiccup! 'Jock' panicked and called Vic's name, then rushed to help the guard. Vic shot the guard again; the bullet went through the guard and into 'Jock'. They were supposed to be professional armed robbers, but it was quickly turning into a farce. Alarm bells rang, sirens wailed and police surrounded the building.

Vic had to decide whether to leave 'Jock' behind or take him with him.

Vic decided to help his friend and pulled his balaclava off. He was hot and sweaty and it felt good to feel the cool air. He picked up his wounded mate and carried him out of the building, armed to the teeth, screaming at police, 'Stand back or I'll shoot!'

He took a policeman hostage and put his mate in the back of the police car. He aimed his gun at the terrified officer's head, then made him drive. The officer was rigid with fear as the car sped off into the distance.

In the ensuing chase, somehow the gun went off, the bullet whizzing past the officer's head. The officer pleaded for his life, 'Don't kill me, please don't kill me.'

Vic wasn't going to kill him. His mind was racing as a million scenarios went through his head; still, killing the Old Bill was the last thing on his mind. The car took off, hell for leather, through the streets of London until they reached leafy suburbia.

The car screeched to a halt outside a secluded house in the middle of nowhere.

Vic made the officer carry his wounded friend towards the house, where he proceeded to kick the door in, much to the surprise of an Irishman called John Stackpoole, who was quietly eating his dinner. There was none of the usual Irish blarney like 'Top of the morning!' or 'Wattleygetcha?' It was more a case of, 'WHAT THE FUCK...?' Vic wasted no words and demanded the keys to the stunned Irishman's car. After bundling his wounded mate and the officer into the motor, he had no choice but to take the Irishman hostage as well.

My jaw dropped open. I gasped, I couldn't believe what he was telling me.

Vic shook his head.

'I know, I know, the whole story sounds fucking unbelievable. But it's true, every single word, and it gets worse...'

As the car sped away at high speed, armed-response units were called and a high-speed chase, accompanied by helicopters, snaked its way across London. It was complete mayhem. The next port of call was a Chinese restaurant, but not for a takeaway – Vic needed a new set of wheels. After several shouts and threats, another hostage joined the not-so-merry day-trippers: a man called Lâm Quang Trân.

The whole thing was gathering speed and momentum like a runaway train. They all had a one-way ticket to nowhere – a fucking nightmare! Vic had to get away – and he had to dump all this excess baggage.

Finally, it all came to a shuddering halt. But not in a station; in a fucking potato field of all places. Vic dumped the hostages and had it away on his toes. He was fully loaded with all guns blazing, the Old Bill in hot pursuit. He made his way to the middle of the field and buried himself under the mud and spuds, with both arms by his sides, holding a gun in each hand. He waited and waited. Police with snarling dogs combed their way through the field, looking for the desperado. Vic never moved a muscle. At one point, an officer stood on Vic's leg; still, he waited. For eight hours he lay in the muddy potato field. But it was a waiting game he inevitably lost.

Vic stood in the dock and was sentenced to forty-eight years behind bars. Forty-eight fucking years for a so-called friend. Vic seethed, 'I should have put one in his nut and saved myself a lot of heartache...'

BACKGROUND

I'm an East Ender, from Forest Gate, Stratford. My dad's Maltese and my mum's English. I've got one brother. I left school and went into engineering, but it wasn't for me.

I met a girl from a place called Wanstead and she took me to her house – it was absolutely beautiful. It was at that point I noticed rich from poor. From that moment on, I decided I didn't want to end up like my dad, working every day that God sends and still ending up saving only a pound a week in the Post Office. That's not knocking my father, it's just not how I wanted to live.

I was always into combat sports: karate, kick-boxing, a little bit of this and a little bit of that. Then I found out about guns and away I went.

I started off robbing building societies when I was seventeen. It was quick and easy money and I loved it.

LIFE OF CRIME

I was twenty years old when I was first put on remand, for stabbing. When I go to prison, I don't get a day off for parole. I go in Category A and come out Category A; I do not concede to the prison system. I've just completed the first of four twelve-year sentences.

WEAPONRY

I've been convicted of stabbing and shooting. Who dares wins!

TOUGHEST MOMENT

My toughest moment was being sentenced to forty-eight years for helping a so-called friend. I took the rap for taking three hostages while on an armed robbery. I could have put a bullet through his head and walked away, but I didn't.

The hardest point was going on a visit and explaining to my family why I gave up my life for a friend. They couldn't understand it. In retrospect, neither can I.

IS THERE ANYONE YOU ADMIRE?

Anyone with good principles. Men of the old school, like Joey Pyle. He's a man of his word.

DO YOU BELIEVE IN CAPITAL PUNISHMENT?

No. Hanging is a terrible way to die. While I was in prison, I found six people hanging in their cells. One inmate, a man called Jimmy Collywood who'd served fourteen years, was in the cell opposite mine and he hanged himself. In the morning I found him. For a time, it affected me badly. The image of Jimmy hanging in his cell, tongue hanging out and eyes bulging, stayed with me for a long time. It's something I'll never forget.

Another reason I don't believe in capital punishment is if an innocent man is hanged. It's no good granting them a pardon if they're dead. There are many innocent men serving life imprisonment for crimes they haven't committed. One that springs to mind is a bloke called Warren Slaney; he's serving life and he is innocent. I've nothing to gain by lying. It's the truth.

IS PRISON A DETERRENT?

No, prison is not a deterrent. When a man commits a crime, especially the act of murder, he doesn't worry about going to prison; he doesn't even think about it.

WHAT WOULD HAVE DETERRED YOU FROM A LIFE OF CRIME?

Money; if I was born into a wealthy family. I never want second-best. I've been chasing money since I was seventeen and I probably always will.

WHAT MAKES A TOUGH GUY?

To get respect, you've got to be nice. If you're a dog, no one likes you. I don't class myself as a nasty person and I don't attack people for nothing, but if you go through the penal system and come through it unscathed, you've got to be fairly tough. It's all right being tough on the streets, but if you've got thirty screws outside your cell, all with riot shields and batons and you're not frightened to steam into them, that sorts the men from the boys.

VIC'S FINAL THOUGHT

I'm not a nasty person. Believe it or not, I've got a conscience; if I was having a row, I would stop if it went too far, but only if I knew I'd won. But if I thought I was going to get a kicking, then I'd take you out of the game.

No question. That's one of the reasons I gave up the guns. If I'm gonna die, I'll take a lot of people with me.

John Daniels

John Daniels is a mountain of a man, an immovable object. He's six four and weighs thirty stone. He looks every bit what he is – Big Bad John.

The first time I saw John Daniels was in March 1995. The reason that date is so prominent in my mind is because it was the day I buried my husband, Ronnie Kray. John was the man assigned to guard Ronnie's body in the Chapel of Rest at Bethnal Green, east London. At the time, I didn't get to speak to John or even acknowledge him; in actual fact, I never saw him again until the day I saw a photograph of him in Nigel Benn's autobiography, *Dark Destroyer*.

Through a friend of a friend, I found out his name and managed to track him down to Luton, Bedfordshire. I telephoned him and explained about the book. John was softly spoken, he wasn't loud, brash or aggressive. He didn't try to be something he wasn't;

he didn't have to. John is what he appears to be – a hard man.

John agreed to meet me and talk, at a pub in Shooter's Hill in south-east London. I've done quite a few interviews at this particular place, but each time I've felt a strange atmosphere there. On this particular day, it was worse. Out of politeness, I asked the lady serving if I could take some photographs in the bar. There was no moment of consideration, just a flat 'no'. I didn't feel that was a problem; it was her pub and she could do what the hell she liked. John eventually had his photographs taken in a subway in south London.

When we returned to the pub to do the interview, I switched on my tape recorder and we started to talk. Almost immediately, music blared from a sound system. It was The Commitments blasting out their version of 'Mustang Sally'. The noise was deafening; we could barely hear ourselves speak. At first, we ignored the loud music. This just irritated the landlady and she turned it up to full volume. We battled on against all odds to do the interview.

Once we'd finished, I thanked John for having driven such a long way and taking part, but also apologised for the way we had been treated. I thought the landlady had made a fool of me – mugged me off – so, before I left, I felt I just had to have a word in her ear.

Leaning nonchalantly on the bar was a middle-aged, peroxide-blonde woman reading a newspaper, fag hanging from the corner of her mouth. I asked if I could

.speak to the landlady. Without looking up from her paper, she spat, 'You're speaking to her.'

Small droplets of saliva cascaded onto the bar. Her very demeanour aggravated me. I asked what the problem was and why had she turned the music up so loud?

'I wanna know what you've been talking about!' she snarled.

I told her it was none of her goddamn business.

'Oh yes it is, it's my pub,' she continued.

I was incensed, absolutely livid. How dare she? What's it got to do with her what we were talking about? I was just about to get out of my pram when, at that moment, John came over and said he was about to leave. I saw the landlady lift her eyes, which instantly widened.

She looked towards Heaven as if she was looking at a skyscraper; the ash fell from her cigarette. John couldn't have chosen a better moment to walk over.

The argument was starting to heat up, but John's sheer presence defused the situation. He gave me a hug and a kiss and said goodbye.

I turned to continue the conversation with the landlady, but she'd lost the sting from her tail; she wasn't sassy any more. I should imagine John has this effect wherever he goes, but he's a bit of an enigma – nobody knows much about him.

BACKGROUND

I've got three brothers and a sister; I'm the middle son. I didn't get into many fights at school because of my size. I've always been big, naturally big. At thirteen years old, I weighed sixteen stone. If I did get into a fight at school, it was generally with older boys.

From leaving school I started minding small clubs and I suppose it was from then on my reputation grew. Nowadays, I spend most of my time as a celebrity bodyguard, both in London and Brooklyn, New York.

LIFE OF CRIME

All the time I've served inside has been for violence; debt-collecting that went over the top or an over-zealous fan of the star I'm minding. I never go out looking for trouble – trouble is my work. It's just part and parcel.

WEAPONRY

My hands. My fists. That's all the weapons I need.

TOUGHEST MOMENT

When my father died. I've known lots of hard men but my father was the hardest I've ever known. Not just because he was my father; he was one tough cookie.

IS THERE ANYONE YOU ADMIRE?

My dad, Joseph. He died eight years ago.

DO YOU BELIEVE IN CAPITAL PUNISHMENT?

That's not just a 'yes' or 'no' answer. I personally do not agree with the death penalty. Having said that, I'm a father and if anyone abused my children I'd kill the perpetrator stone-dead. It doesn't make it right, but that's what I'd do. An eye for an eye. But capital punishment is cold-blooded murder and that's wrong – it's a civilised society killing someone for killing.

IS PRISON A DETERRENT?

No. Track record proves it. Look how many prisoners are repeat offenders.

WHAT WOULD HAVE DETERRED YOU FROM A LIFE OF CRIME?

To be honest, I don't think anything would have deterred me. Most people in my world would be in it no matter what. It's partly circumstances and also the make-up of that person.

WHAT MAKES A TOUGH GUY?

A man who doesn't use violence for violence's sake. Like when you see a bouncer on a door – a big guy, who has a reputation to match – then a five-foot-high drunken office worker abuses him. The doorman stays cool; he knows he can take him out at any time but he doesn't, instead he tells him to run along and saves it for another day. If he was to take advantage of the situation and bash the office worker, that would make the big guy a bully, not a tough guy. How I see it, if someone is drunk and can barely stand, there's no glory in bashing him up. I don't have anything to prove. Little dogs bark, big dogs bite!

BIG JOHN'S FINAL THOUGHT

I've had more than my fair share of fights, but I evaluate every situation. There have been circumstances where I've been outnumbered three to one; it's then I make my judgement. Are they going to go away without a fight? If I come to the conclusion they're not, then I'll lash out first. I usually come out on top. I would fight to the death if I had to, it doesn't matter how outnumbered I am, I will go forward. I've never gone down. My father always said to me, 'If you're going forward when you go down, then you've won ...'

Cornish Mick

Normally, when a man reaches a certain age or when his beer-gut swells, he seeks out a personal trainer. But not Cornish Mick. In his younger, thinner days, he used to do a bit of boxing. He's from the school of hard knocks and is a little bit 'tasty'. Mick tenderly pats his beer belly and winks, then holds up his right index finger and smiles. 'That's all I need. It takes one finger to pull a trigger.'

Mick can't be bothered with all the puffing and panting, sweat and toil from training down the gym. He's not a man who'll waste words or make idle threats – no matter how big a man is, he just lets his finger do the talking.

He's a cutter; a shooter; a killer. Upset him and he'll pop a cap in your arse and bury you in the woods sooner than look at you. I know – I have first-hand experience of Mick's bad temper.

It was late Saturday night. Yet another gangster do. Men in hand-made dinner suits. Villains' wives, all lipstick, powder and paint. I sat at the top table with the top men, all smoking the best Cuban Lah-di-dahs.

Mick sat beside me. We chatted and laughed about this and that, until a big man in a cheap suit started making a bit of a nuisance of himself. He was a wannabe gangster, a loudmouth with nothing to say and saying it too loud.

I remember thinking, with a foolish sense of annoyance, that I wished the geezer would just go away. Mick's eyes narrowed. There was no mistaking that he was beginning to get irritable.

Mick was no longer listening to what I was saying; his mind elsewhere. The loud-mouthed plastic gangster was clearly getting on his nerves.

Mick stood up, shrugged his shoulders and straightened his tie. His eyes looked spiteful. I had never seen him like this before. He walked over to the geezer and told him to fuck off. Mick said it with conviction. Then he said it with some scorn. The loudmouth spluttered and stammered, 'Err ... Err ...'

Suddenly, from his back pocket, Mick pulled out a blade. The loudmouth was no longer loud. With no more words, no more warnings, Mick dragged the blade slowly down the man's cheek.

The man's eyes widened to the size of saucers as he clutched his face. Blood, the colour of fine red Chianti, trickled through his fingers. Mick pulled a crisp white handkerchief from the top pocket of his bespoke suit and handed it to the man. Then he coolly hailed a cab. He helped the man into the taxi with as much concern as a scorned woman. Mick turned to me, 'Sorry, Kate, where was we?'

BACKGROUND

I was born in Cornwall. There's nothing much to say about Cornwall except that the pasties are nice! The eldest son of two brothers and two sisters. My dad was in the Army most of the time so the discipline was left to my mother, and I must say she was a dab hand with a broom handle!

I came to London when I was forty-two years old, after I'd been round the world doing various naughty things. I followed my heart, and a girl, to London. The romance didn't last long. When I got some 'bird', she pissed off with someone else. Ah well, you can't win 'em all. But I stayed in London – on business, of course!

LIFE OF CRIME

I've been away for eighteen years altogether, but have been sentenced to about thirty-five, most of which were for crimes of violence and armed robbery.

WEAPONRY

I only need one finger to beat the biggest man in the world – my trigger finger.

TOUGHEST MOMENT

Losing my dad, I think, was the toughest moment in my life. He died in 1963 when I was in Dartmoor. The screw unlocked my cell and told me straight that my dad had died. I couldn't even get a day out for the funeral.

IS THERE ANYONE YOU ADMIRE?

Joey Pyle. He's a fair man, he's loyal, he'll stick to his guns and he won't turn anyone over. What you see is what you get with Joe.

DO YOU BELIEVE IN CAPITAL PUNISHMENT?

For crimes against women and children – yes, I do.

IS PRISON A DETERRENT?

While you're young it's not, the consequences just go over your head. You don't think about getting caught or else you wouldn't do the crime. Every thief in the country believes he will never get caught – someone else, but never him.

I know some of the hardest men around who cry themselves to sleep because they just cannot stand being locked up. Then there's people like Reggie Kray and Ronnie Fields. They don't do it easy, they do it the best way they can. When you get to a certain age, you look back and think about everything you've missed and start to think twice. I'm sixty-five now. I don't want any more bird.

WHAT MAKES A TOUGH GUY?

Pride is a part of it. If you've got pride in yourself, there's no way you'll be made a mug of. It's not muscular development or anything like that. I know little blokes that are as hard as nails. I think it's pride and having a sense of right and wrong. If somebody does you wrong, then you've got to do something about it. It's hard to put into words. You can have a bloke as big as a house that can't hold his hands up because he just hasn't got the heart. Having a heart plays a big part in being a tough guy.

MICK'S FINAL THOUGHT

I don't feel in danger in my local pub just having a quiet drink. But there are times when I go out and stand with my back to the bar and watch certain people all night. To me, Roy Shaw is one of those. Although he's straight with his mates, if I didn't know him I'd be very, very careful. I think it's the unpredictability of some people's nature. Ronnie Kray would fly into a rage for no apparent reason, like swearing in front of a lady. Roy Shaw is exactly the same. Something would snap in him if he thought you were taking the piss. You can say what you like to me, but if you take the piss or if I thought my life was in danger or I was going to get nicked, I'd kill you – no hesitation.

Charlie Bronson

I visited Charlie Bronson – the most dangerous prisoner in the penal system – at Woodhill Prison, Milton Keynes. Woodhill is a top-security prison and has a specially designed unit for men with no release date and nothing to lose. It's a prison within a prison, known as Britain's Alcatraz.

Charlie has spent twenty-six years out of the last thirty in solitary confinement in prisons like Woodhill. He has been locked in dungeons, in iron boxes concreted into the middle of cells and, famously, in a cage like the fictional Hannibal Lecter. He has endured more periods of isolation than any other living British prisoner, spending months at a time with nothing more than cockroaches for company. He is always held under maximum security, in a spartan cell with little more than a fireproof bed and a table and chair made from

41

compressed cardboard. When he's unlocked, up to twelve prison officers – sometimes in riot gear and with dogs – are standing by.

I arrived for my visit half an hour early. I parked my car and went to the reception desk, told them my name and gave them my passport for identification.

I wasn't told to sit with the other prison visitors, but was shown into a small, secure room. An officer handed me a piece of paper with a number on and motioned his head towards a large tray. I was then told to remove my jacket, shoes and watch ready to be searched. I passed through an X-ray machine identical to the ones you find at airports. I was then asked to move to another area and stand on a special box with both my arms out in order to be searched.

I was asked to open my mouth and lift my tongue. An officer looked in my ears and up my nose, then felt under my arms, around my chest and down my body. I had to lift my feet so that they could examine in between my toes. I was then told to lean back and toss my hair forward. I asked what they were looking for – concealed drugs and weapons. Eventually, I was given back the tray containing my possessions and permission was granted for me to continue to the next gate accompanied by three officers.

'Lima two six, lima two six, permission to walk?' whispered one of the officers into a small radio. Each step of the way was the same; at each gate, permission had to be granted before we could move on. I was led into the final reception area, where I was thoroughly searched for the second time.

The only thing I was allowed to take into the inner sanctums of the prison was a bag of loose change for the vending machines. Charlie had left a list for me; he wanted six chocolate bars and four bottles of Buxton spring water. I had awful trouble with the vending machines, it was taking such a long time. An officer came in and said that Charlie was getting agitated and they would sort his shopping list out for me later.

I continued my journey through the prison; surveillance cameras followed my every move. I was spooked by the eerie silence. Two huge male officers opened a small room containing two long tables. One table had one chair on one side and three chairs on the other. Sitting at the other table were four officers.

They stood up as Charlie was brought in. He was wearing a chequered pea-green and canary-yellow boiler suit. He had a shaven head and a beard down to his naval – oh, and little round sunglasses like John Lennon used to wear. Charlie smiled; so did I. A puzzled look came across his face and he asked in a gruff voice, 'Are they your real teef?'

I put on my best smile and replied, 'Yeah.'

Charlie walked towards me, and suddenly the officers were on high alert.

'Can I tap 'em?'

I exposed my pearly gates for him to tap. Gently, with his finger, he proceeded to tap my teeth, one by one.

'Ooh, lovely,' he cooed. 'Sit down, let's have a chat.'

We settled down in the small, cramped room. Six officers, Charlie Bronson and me. This is what he said.

BACKGROUND

I have two brothers – John and Mark. My childhood was like any other – 'mad'!

LIFE OF CRIME

I've been in prison for twenty-six years. I'm still Category A. I hold the record for the longest-serving prisoner in solitary confinement – twenty-two years. I'm currently kept in a cage naked and fed through a cat flap.

WEAPONRY

My most dangerous weapon is my madness and unpredictability. I have a problem where I just change in a spin and become something that's not human. I'm not really a wicked man but put an axe in my hand and I'll show you an abattoir.

TOUGHEST MOMENT

Holding a guy by his feet from a balcony eighteen floors up and deciding whether to let go. I pulled him in. I regret it because the man's a rat. Maybe next time!

IS THERE ANYONE YOU ADMIRE?

My medicine ball – Bertha.

DO YOU BELIEVE IN CAPITAL PUNISHMENT?

Yes, all paedophiles should hang. There is no cure for them. Kids are innocent and scum who kill them should be hung.

IS PRISON A DETERRENT?

No, prison is not a deterrent. How can it be? Prison breeds tougher villains.

WHAT WOULD HAVE DETERRED YOU FROM A LIFE OF CRIME?

Love, understanding and apple pies!

WHAT MAKES A TOUGH GUY?

Feelings and fairness. A man's got to have them, or he's not a man. Without feelings you're a mutant.

CHARLIE'S FINAL THOUGHT

I was in Broadmoor for the criminally insane in a dormitory and Gordon Robinson was in the next bed. He was bugging me. I'd hit the fucking idiot once before, but I knew our paths would cross again, and there he was in the next bed.

My mother and father had just been to see me; I was feeling happy. After the visit I went back to the ward and found Robinson with his key in my locker. The toerag was trying to open it. A locker thief! Prison rule number one – do not steal from other cons. I pushed him away, then I chinned him. But that wasn't enough for me; I wanted to kill him. He deserved to die; he was going to die.

I've got a silver tie that my dad had given me some years ago. My favourite tie. I locked myself in the toilet and tested its strength on the toilet cistern. To my surprise, it held my weight. I decided to strangle Gordon Robinson that very night. I was excited. It was the same buzz I got from doing armed robberies. I walked into the dormitory in my pyjamas with the tie round my waist, out of sight. I climbed into bed and waited.

Robinson's left eye was almost closed from where I punched him earlier. His other eye was alert. I smiled my best smile.

The night patrol nurse looked in every half an hour through the observation slit in the door. I only needed a couple of minutes. Fuck the night watchman! There was no saving the thief. I lay still, deep in thought, the tie wrapped around my wrist under the blankets, just waiting. Like a spider waits for the fly. Time was plentiful, I had all night long. This was my night, my fly – I was buzzing. Twelve o'clock, one o'clock, I waited patiently watching every bed, every movement. Then it happened, as if I'd sent the thief a telepathic message. He moved. He sat up. He bent over to put his slippers on. He was probably going for a piss.

I leapt out of bed. In a second the tie was wrapped

around his ugly neck. I was strangling the locker thief! It felt magic, it felt right. Surprisingly, there was very little noise – a sigh, a groan at first, then nothing. I pulled tighter, and leant over to watch. His eyes bulged, his face went grey, his tongue protruded. Dribble ran from the corner of his mouth. He pissed himself, I smelt shit. He was on his way out of planet earth. Then it happened; the tie snapped. I had half the tie in one hand and half in the other. He began making noises, loud animal grunts, deep chesty moans. Other patients began to stir. Now I was in trouble. I acted fast; I punched him in the face and straddled him. I shouted to the loons that he was having a nightmare, but the purple welts around his neck told their story.

I spent the next four years in Broadmoor's hellhole – the punishment blocks – and I never got the opportunity to strangle Gordon Robinson again!

Freddie Foreman

Freddie Foreman resembles the sinister character of Mr Christie from the notorious horror film, *10 Rillington Place*. He's softly spoken. His eyes stare unblinkingly. He's a man who has done what he's done and doesn't give a fuck who knows it!

One of the things that I didn't know was that it was Freddie Foreman who was with Reggie Kray when Ronnie died, on St Patrick's Day in 1995. Freddie was in Maidstone prison when he was told that Ron had died. When he heard the news of Ronnie's untimely death he asked to be taken on to Reggie's wing to comfort him. As soon as Reggie saw Fred, he burst into tears and hugged him. Fred comforted Reg the best he could.

They had a long friendship that stretched over more than forty years. A jug of green hooch appeared from another friend and Fred stayed with Reg all day. They talked of the old days and of fond memories of Ron.

The inmates kept them supplied with more jugs of green stuff.

They weren't hungry, but sandwiches came by the platefuls – tuna, ham – and more green stuff. The old friends stayed together for a day and a night. Reg asked Fred to be a pallbearer at Ronnie's funeral.

When Fred told me this story some five years later while I was interviewing him for this book, his voice cracked with emotion. I saw Freddie Foreman with a tear in his eye as he remembered his old friend. Who says that tough men don't cry?

BACKGROUND
I am one of five brothers – Wally, Herbie, George and Bert. All of us are products of the war years. Unlike my brothers, I was too young to serve in the Army, so I lived off my wits and thieved off the pavement. By the time I was eighteen, I'd become a full-time thief. My social life was exciting and fulfilling and I was fit and ready to take on the world.

LIFE OF CRIME
I've been sentenced to twenty years in prison for murder and disposing of a body, but have served fourteen years.

WEAPONRY

I was a professional boxer and had over forty professional fights. So I would say that I can have a 'straightener', but I prefer to use a gun.

TOUGHEST MOMENT

On my birthday, I was sentenced to ten years for disposing of Jack 'The Hat' McVitie's body. I was taken to the cells beneath the court and given another ten years for murdering Frank 'the Mad Axeman' Mitchell. I'd say that was a tough moment and a pretty shit birthday!

IS THERE ANYONE YOU ADMIRE?

Ed Bunker, who served twenty years behind bars in America. He played Mr Blue in the film *Reservoir Dogs*. Once released from prison, he didn't just blend into the background, he got on with his life and became a successful writer, writing magnificent books like *Runaway Train* and *Dog Eat Dog*.

DO YOU BELIEVE IN CAPITAL PUNISHMENT?

No, definitely not. It's been proven that innocent men have gone to the gallows. Perverts and child abusers should not be hanged, they should be chopped up and fed to the dogs. Myself, I would like to take them fishing.

IS PRISON A DETERRENT?

No. Prison is a breeding ground for crime, but what else is there? Short, sharp shock treatment is a good idea.

National Service was a good idea; tagging another. I think the answer today is to educate kids. Ninety per cent of tearaways can't read or write.

Once the hormones start kicking in, we have a problem. Testosterone is a powerful thing. If we shake up our education system and revise the National Curriculum, then perhaps things will change.

WHAT WOULD HAVE DETERRED YOU FROM A LIFE OF CRIME?

A good education. It would have been easier to earn money the straight way rather than the crooked – less hazardous.

WHAT MAKES A TOUGH GUY?

Tough guys are a rare breed. But when you come across a real tough man, you've no doubt. They are courteous and polite, not loud and full of veiled threats. You sense their danger; can almost taste it. A smiling viper!

FREDDIE'S FINAL THOUGHT

Old professional criminals don't exist any more – Maggie Thatcher took care of that. She gave the police a licence to shoot armed criminals in certain circumstances. While she was in government, more armed robbers were shot dead than at any other time. Modern technology has taken care of the rest – surveillance cameras are everywhere.

Nowadays, most crime is drug-related. Petty crimes by petty criminals. Drugs frazzle brains, leaving the person with no morals or standards. I'm one of the old school where there was honour amongst thieves. When I was at it, I wouldn't have dreamt of burgling a neighbour's house. It was the 'haves and have-nots'. I'd target big banks, post offices and security companies. I'd never hurt the normal man in the street; I'd only hurt other gangsters if they did me a wrong or crossed me in my line of business.

Sure, I've gunned down quite a few men throughout my life – Frank Mitchell and Ginger Marks, to name but two – but I don't regret murdering them one bit. After killing them, I wrapped them up in chicken wire attached to weights and buried them far out at sea, away from fishing lanes, deep beneath the cold, muddy waters of the English Channel. I'd been told by an American friend that bodies weighed down in this way would never find their way to the surface but would slowly be devoured by crabs and other deep-sea creatures.

There has always been great speculation and mystery surrounding the demise of Jack The Hat, Frank Mitchell and Ginger Marks, and how their bodies were disposed of. Only a few people – perhaps a handful of close friends – knew that it was me that took them on a fishing trip!

The only regret I've got in my life is that I'd like to have killed a couple more men, but, lucky for them and unfortunately for me, I missed 'em! Oh yeah, and the other regret I've got is being caught. Must dash, I'm going fishing!

Bill

Bill's hair is short and spiky, a chaotic mix of styles that blends into one hip hairdo.

'I ask myself,' he says, plopping down into a leather Chesterfield armchair in his jeweller's shop in east London, 'what the fuck am I doing here? Why do you wanna interview me? I ain't no hard man!'

I smiled a nervous smile. 'I beg to differ, Bill.'

How can a man that looks like Bill say he's not a hard man? If ever a man's face told a story, then Bill's is a novel. His combat boots and trousers scream, 'VIOLENCE, VIOLENCE, VIOLENCE!' His fists are like club hammers; his stubby arms are built like well-oiled machine tools, ever pumping and grinding. The impression Bill makes is that if you were stupid enough to hit him over the head with a bottle, it would have about as much effect as the champagne magnum that launched the *QEII*. His voice booms with authority.

When he says, 'sit', not only the dog in the room sits, so does everybody else. Let's face it, if you saw Bill in a dark alley walking his dog, would you be comfortable walking past him, or would your heart pound that little bit faster? Let's say it how it is – Bill is one mean mother-fucker. No ifs, buts or maybes.

Life is full of surprises. It wasn't until halfway through our interview that it dawned on Bill my name was Kray. To our amazement, I discovered that years ago, Bill used to visit Ron in Broadmoor. I met many people while I was married to Ron, all of whom played some part in the murky depths of the underworld – murderers, bank robbers and villains of all shapes and sizes, including yardies. If they'd been to visit Ron, they would have been up to no good and involved in some kind of naughty business. Put it this way – they certainly wouldn't have been straight-up geezers.

Once Bill and I had established that he'd been a friend of Ron's, he became more relaxed and opened up. He spoke warmly of Ron and, from the way he spoke and the things he said, I knew that he had at one time been a good friend to Ron. It's a small world.

I'd never met or heard of Bill but he'd been recommended to me for the book by the 'highest authority'. He had come with the glowing reference of being one of Britain's hardest bastards. As the interview progressed, I slowly peeled away the hard coating that Bill had built up over the years to protect himself. There was layer upon layer of animosity and anger. As we stripped away the protective shell, there were times he had difficulty in expressing himself. The top and bottom of it is that he's a violent, angry young man – full-stop.

Bill smiled – a rare smile. For a moment, his face changed. It was no longer hostile, it was as if someone had turned a light on in his eyes.

'Well, Kate, if you say I'm a hard man, then I guess I am!'

BACKGROUND

I was brought up in Whitechapel, east London. Then my family moved to south London. I've got two brothers and two sisters. I'm the eldest boy. I was bit of a nuisance at school but nothing out of the ordinary. My parents were fairly strict. I had a good upbringing but I wasn't over-privileged or anything like that. I suppose from day one I was getting myself into problems, but I was just mischievous. Although Mum didn't see it like that; she was always up the school for one thing or another.

To keep me off the streets, more than anything, I started training and body-building – not for competition reasons, just for the sake of keeping fit.

I had a period when I didn't keep fit and I went up to twenty-eight stone, had a sixty-four-inch waist and I could hardly walk or breathe. I didn't like that feeling and have never stopped training since. I'm fitter and more agile at my present weight of twenty-three stone.

LIFE OF CRIME

I've been to prison once and that was enough for me. I've done lots of bad things and never been caught for them. Ironically, I did time for a relatively minor offence. A policeman was taking pictures of me and all I did was take the film out of his camera!

When I got banged up, I thought to myself, this ain't me, this is not a clever place to be, and no matter what it takes, I never intend doing any more 'bird'.

WEAPONRY

I can never tell what situation I'm gonna be in. I like to use my fists if I have to, but I will always try to avoid violence. Unfortunately, I've got a bit of a temper, so anything could happen. I'm not frightened to use tools and have done in the past, but it depends whether it warrants it or not. I never commit violence unnecessarily. I'm not one of these guys who'll use my position to bully people.

In my view, bullies always come unstuck. My motto in life is: 'The man who's frightened is the man you've got to be careful of!' He knows he's got to take you out of the game, because if he doesn't, he knows he will die. Simple!

TOUGHEST MOMENT

When I went to New Orleans, I had a little confrontation with the Ku Klux Klan. I was on holiday with my girlfriend, and we were having a wonderful time.

BILL

We went to the Grand Cayman, then to Disney World, and we ended up in New Orleans for the Mardi Gras.

While thumbing through some brochures in the hotel lobby, we saw an advert for an Island Swamp Tour. My fascination with alligators got the better of me and, spontaneously, we booked two tickets for the following day.

The sun was hot as we waited to board the small boat to take us into the swamp. A ranger took our tickets and, as he did, I noticed tattooed on his hand the letters KKK – Ku Klux Klan. The ranger didn't acknowledge me; in fact, he didn't even look in my direction. He just turned his back and started speaking into a small radio.

'We got a n****r on board the boat...'

By now I was getting bad vibes. But I thought, fuck it, I've paid my money to see the alligators, I'm just gonna go. At that moment, I didn't realise just what danger I was in. I looked round the boat and there was a sea of white faces – it was only then it dawned on me how serious the situation was.

As we set off through the swamp, the ranger went through the motions of 'the helpful tour guide' and passed snapshots around the boat. When he got to me, for the first time we had eye contact. 'Pass it over, boy,' he hissed.

The ranger could see I was no mug and I wouldn't back down. He didn't argue, in fact he never said a word. He just turned the boat round and headed back to shore.

As I stepped off the boat, there were twelve armed sheriffs waiting for me. I was in trouble – big fucking trouble. I wasn't in London, I was in New Orleans, America's Deep South, where black men are lynched. All of them wanted a slice of my black ass. I'm not ashamed to say, but I was scared. Man, was I scared.

'Hey, boy,' one of the officers asked in a slow American drawl, 'are you that man on the telly, Mr T?'

My mind was racing and my heart pounded.

'Er ... er ... yeah, that's right, I'm Mr T...'

For the first time in my life, I was happy to be mistaken for this character.

The mood changed. He actually asked me for an autograph for his kids. Then he warned me, 'I trust you won't be round these parts again. People go missing round here, BOY.'

I got my black ass out of there as quick as possible because there was no doubt they were definitely gonna have some fun with me.

IS THERE ANYONE YOU ADMIRE?
God.

DO YOU BELIEVE IN CAPITAL PUNISHMENT?
I do believe in hanging for perverts but, saying that, there can be no mistakes.

IS PRISON A DETERRENT?

To the majority, I don't think it is a deterrent. In fact, if you go to jail, you become more knowledgeable about crime. You're associating with criminals, so what do you expect? To some people, one bit of 'bird' is more than enough. In my case, I felt like a caged animal. I'm not saying that if I had to go to prison I wouldn't be able to do the 'bird', because I know I can. It's just something I'd rather avoid.

WHAT WOULD HAVE DETERRED YOU FROM A LIFE OF CRIME?

Nothing would have deterred me. It's not something I planned to do, it just happened. If I need money or whatever, I'll do what I have to do. It's just survival.

WHAT MAKES A TOUGH GUY?

A man who tries to avoid violence and doesn't use unnecessary force. I believe in warning people first. If that doesn't work, I say, 'In the name of God, man, think carefully, you don't fucking want this!' I always quote God's name. But there's always one who wants to push it.

Respect – if a man hasn't got that, he's got fuck all. Then I have no choice, I take him out.

BILL'S FINAL THOUGHT

Racism has come a long way. There is still institutionalised racism, but that will always be there; you've got to accept that. People will always have their views, no matter what.

If people make comments about my colour, the way I react depends on the situation; whether I'm with my girlfriend, my kids or whether it's worth the fucking bother.

Sometimes I have to wipe my mouth; I think it's harder for a man to wipe his mouth than to kill someone. Taking someone's life isn't an easy thing to live with, I don't care how hard you think you are. That's the worst regret I've got. They've got families, it's not just you it affects. It leaves a trail of shit behind. Murder – it's a messy business!

Harry H

Harry is 'quintessentially English'. The 'Lovely Harry', as his mates call him, is as English as black cabs, double-decker buses and red telephone boxes. He wears finely tailored Savile Row suits and Fratelli Rossetti crocodile shoes. He carries an ivory cane and has perfect double cuffs, which he adjusts at regular intervals. He's today's David Niven or Trevor Howard.

Harry possesses a taste for the good life and a sense of mischief that no true English gent is complete without. Whether it's driving around in Jaguars and Rollers or eating 'speed' like it's going out of fashion, he takes his pleasures wherever he can. He sails through life without leaving a shambles behind; behaving reasonably well, being honest, a man of his word and, not least, having a good time.

But Harry was born with a streak of mischief running through him. He's not your average nine-to-five man, never has been and never will be. He likes to think of himself as an entrepreneur who will, on impulse, try anything once.

Nowadays, he tells me that he's given up the 'dirty rat race'. But like the true English gentleman that he is, he's retired to a quintessential cottage in the country, with quintessential roses around the door, a quintessentially wire-haired fox terrier by his side, and an all-singing, all-dancing, waving, African grey parrot called Claude, who Harry has taught to stutter.

Harry adjusts his cuffs and straightens his tie for the last time during our interview. He lovingly hands Claude a monkey nut while trying to convince me that he's retired and is now a virtual recluse. Claude interrupts with a squawk and a screech, 'He's a g-g-g-good boy now!'

BACKGROUND

I was born and brought up in the Garden of England – Kent. I have an older brother and an older sister. I was a normal kid from a normal family. I looked up to my father; he was a good man. My mother was the disciplinarian; she tried her best, bless her heart. I've always been a loner, I find it better that way. If I don't trust anyone then I won't be let down. I think it was my destiny to be a rascal. Even from the age of thirteen I was heading down the wrong road, when I was busted for drugs.

LIFE OF CRIME
Nothing to speak of – only drugs, firearms and fraud!

WEAPONRY
When I was younger, I was hot-headed and would have a tear-up with anyone. Now I'm older, I realise there is more than one way to skin a cat!

TOUGHEST MOMENT
Realising my thirteen-year marriage had fallen apart.

IS THERE ANYONE YOU ADMIRE?
Great leaders, like Churchill. He was a strong man, a leader of his time.

DO YOU BELIEVE IN CAPITAL PUNISHMENT?
No. If we are to believe that taking someone's life is evil, then it's evil across the board. Society is wrong to take a life. They are as guilty as the person they are trying.

IS PRISON A DETERRENT?
Like a lot of things, prison is only a deterrent until you've experienced it. It's fear of the unknown.

WHAT WOULD HAVE DETERRED YOU FROM A LIFE OF CRIME?
A family.

WHAT MAKES A TOUGH GUY?

To me, a tough guy is a man who believes in something enough to kill or be killed. Great men like Malcolm X, the Irishman Michael Collins and the Scot William Wallace. They all died for a cause they truly believed in.

HARRY'S FINAL THOUGHT

The first thing a man should take into consideration before embarking on a life of crime is his family and his loved ones. Also, honour, pride, self-respect and his word are all-important. A man is nothing if he's not true to his word. It's not easy to take another man's life. I know from experience you'll never be the same person, no matter who you are. Everyone has a conscience.

Joey Pyle

Joey Pyle is the archetypal gangster, like the Godfather, Don Corleone. He wouldn't look out of place in movies like *The Long Good Friday* or *Goodfellas*. Joey has ruled the roost in the underworld for more than four decades. He is the original 'Teflon Don' – nothing sticks.

Each and every man I interviewed for this book had either known or heard of Joey Pyle. He is the most respected of them all. I've never heard anyone say a bad word about him; whether that's through fear or admiration, I'm really not sure. Either way, he's held in the highest esteem by everyone.

The beauty of Joey Pyle is that he has the capability of mixing in any circles, whether it be royalty, celebrities, MPs or murderers. He's at ease with them all. Maybe it's this quality that has given him longevity in the underworld. He is a man of few words, a shrewd businessman, someone you'd be reluctant to approach without an introduction. His very size and presence are enough to make you take a step back.

His hair is black, slicked back with grey around the sides, making him appear very distinguished. Remove his dark sunglasses and they reveal twinkling blue eyes that are soft around women and cold as ice to men.

He has the ability to hold everyone at arm's length and you're only in Joey's company if you're invited. No problem is too big for Joe and he can minimise any problem with just a word or wave of his hand. Wherever he goes, he is well-respected, but only a fool would take his kindness as a weakness.

BACKGROUND

I was brought up in Islington, the eldest of four children. The greatest influence in my life was my dad's twin brother, Joe. He was the ABA and Amateur Welterweight champion of Great Britain. As a child I used to watch him box and loved every minute of it. Inevitably, I followed in his footsteps and started boxing at twelve years old at the Angel in Islington. Boxing came easy to me and I was bloody good it at it as well. I won loads of trophies, eventually becoming the schoolboy boxing champion of Surrey. I'd won all there was to win as an amateur so therefore turned professional. I had twenty-two fights as a professional boxer. I lost my first and last fight to a boxer named Maxie Beach. It was at that moment I decided to become a gangster instead of a fighter.

LIFE OF CRIME

I have always been a bit of a rascal. In 1955, when I was eighteen, I did my first 'screwer' [burglary]. It was a TA hall and I was stunned when I walked away with seven grand in my pocket. Seven fucking grand, what a result!

It was the easiest money I've ever earned. This gave me the taste for hard cash and started me on the road to a life of crime. I've never looked back since. Over the following years I thieved 'on the pavement', which is the polite way of describing pillage and plunder. It got me into all sorts of trouble.

In all, I've been arrested fifty times and have been sentenced to thirty-five years in prison. I've spent fifteen years behind bars. I've been tried at the Old Bailey, Court Number One four times: for robbery, drug smuggling and murder. But each time I've been found 'not guilty', of course.

WEAPONRY

My brain is my biggest weapon.

TOUGHEST MOMENT

The hardest battle was seeing my mother die in September 1999. Her death knocked me for six, it was as if something inside me fell on its side.

IS THERE ANYONE YOU ADMIRE?

Joe Louis, nicknamed 'The Brown Bomber', the greatest boxer that ever lived.

DO YOU BELIEVE IN CAPITAL PUNISHMENT?

No. If one innocent person is hung, then the system
is wrong.

IS PRISON A DETERRENT?

No – but what else is there? Prison is not meant as a
deterrent, prison is meant as a punishment.

WHAT WOULD HAVE DETERRED YOU FROM A LIFE OF
CRIME?

Nothing or no one would have deterred me.

WHAT MAKES A TOUGH GUY?

It's not the size of a man, nor his stature, but his heart
and his principles. A man could be four feet tall, but if he
is a man of his word he gains respect from those around
him. Only then does he become a tough guy.

JOEY'S FINAL THOUGHT

I've no remorse, no conscience and no regrets for the
things I've done in my life. The one thing I've always
believed is that a still tongue keeps a wise head. If you
gamble with the Devil, the Devil will win.

Frasier
Tranter

Frasier Tranter is a big bloke. In fact, he's gigantic in size, height, weight and power. Fortunately, as I'm in the iron grip of his huge handshake, I realise I'm standing slightly down a slope from him and he is, in fact, only six feet ten, not the nine feet it seems.

I'd waited four months to interview Frasier. Each time I phoned him to ask when he was in London, it was always the same answer:

'My wife is pregnant. I don't want to leave her.'

Most thirty-five-year-old blokes with film-star looks are concentrating on getting pissed and pulling the Lycra-clad blonde dancing round her handbag in Stringfellows. But not Frasier; he's an amiable and down-to-earth bloke who likes nothing more than spending time with his family in Wolverhampton and training – that is, when he's not taking calls on the telephone, something he did a lot throughout our interview. Frasier bristled with pride and smiled one of those new father smiles.

'My wife gave birth to a baby boy. I've got a son. I'm a dad.'

Mention tough guys and his face changes dramatically.

'I don't like gangsters,' he sneers.

Whoops! I was unsure if he knew that I was a Kray. If he didn't like gangsters then he was talking to the wrong person. Tentatively, I asked him if he knew who I'd been married to.

'Oh, yeah, the Krays. They're different ...'

I'm not sure how or why Frasier thought that Reg and Ron were different to any other. They were gangsters and murderers, which epitomises everything that he despises. Nevertheless, Frasier is a tough guy – a straight, tough guy.

Throughout our interview he made his views on criminals crystal clear and insisted that he was not a hard man. We had a long discussion on what makes a hard man. We both agreed that bullies are not tough guys; they are just bullies. Some men are naturally tough, with an inner strength and sense of pride and dignity, like himself. He can't and won't, for some reason, let anyone push him around or take a liberty with him, but that doesn't make him a bully. Still, Frasier protested, saying he wasn't a hard man.

At the photoshoot later, Don the photographer asked Frasier to behave like he was in a strongman competition; to gesture angrily and shout. Frasier shouted for the camera and gritted his teeth, 'Come on! Come on!'

Everyone who was training in the gym stopped what they were doing and watched the big fella. Don continued to egg him on; Frasier responded. His eyes bulged. Purple veins in his neck swelled, pumping blood to his brain.

He grimaced, face contorted with the effort. His face glistened with sweat. Two skinny lads watched from the back of the gym. One nudged the other: 'I wouldn't like to upset him. He's one hard bastard.'

BACKGROUND

I'm from Wolverhampton. I don't want to talk about my childhood. All I will say is that my parents were divorced and when I left school I had several menial jobs before starting work on the doors.

LIFE OF CRIME

I'm squeaky clean.

WEAPONRY

Being a strongman, I have to be strong all over. I can't have any weak points. My strength is in my back and shoulders.

TOUGHEST MOMENT

The biggest challenge of my life was in The World's Strongest Man competition in Morocco in 1998. I was a late entry and only had four weeks to prepare. Some guy from Denmark dropped out and I was put in at short notice. From the moment I stepped off the plane in Morocco, I felt intimidated by the other contestants. Their sheer size and strength was awesome. I didn't do very well, but at least I tried. Hopefully I'll win The World's Strongest Man 2000.

IS THERE ANYONE YOU ADMIRE?

Martine McCutcheon – Tiffany from *EastEnders*. She's gorgeous. I'd give up everything for her.

DO YOU BELIEVE IN CAPITAL PUNISHMENT?

No, in case of mistakes. I believe people suffer more in prison. Take Myra Hindley as an example; I believe she suffered more by being incarcerated for more than three decades.

IS PRISON A DETERRENT?

I don't know, I've never been. If people are a danger to society then they have to be segregated from it.

WHAT WOULD HAVE DETERRED YOU FROM A LIFE OF CRIME?

Prison. Any man that says prison is a 'doddle' is a fool.

WHAT MAKES A TOUGH GUY?

A man that can walk away from a fight rather than get involved.

FRASIER'S FINAL THOUGHT

I've been pushed to the limit several times and have lashed out. I don't particularly enjoy violence but I'm not going to stand there and be a punch bag for anyone. Some people look at me and think that, because I'm big, I'm a target. Everybody has a tolerance level. Sometimes it's a long fuse and sometimes it's not. Every man has a limit and when you're pushed to that limit, no matter how big or small you are, you will lash out. An angry man is a dangerous man!

Errol
Francis

Meeting Errol Francis was an extraordinary experience. What did I expect? An awesome, frightening bodyguard perhaps? A larger-than-life, in-your-face bully type? Whatever I expected, what I actually got was a surprise. Quite a lot of surprises, actually.

The first thing that struck me was his shyness. Errol is an extremely modest and reserved man. He is smaller than I'd expected, but much broader than I'd imagined. In actual fact, he's colossal – a whopping monster of a man. Even more of a surprise is that his size is natural. Errol doesn't use any growth-enhancing substances like steroids. His bulk is just the result of pure hard work and clean-living. He's not a man who goes out boozing with his mates or womanising. Errol is a family man. His wife Sandra and their children come before anything or anybody. That was evident the first time I met him.

The other thing I didn't expect was his warmth. On our first, brief meeting, he grabbed my hand and shook it like he really was genuinely pleased to see me, before ushering me into a room where 'we could talk'.

Errol found it difficult speaking about himself and his many achievements. I had to coax every single word from him. It was a long, drawn-out process and Errol said he'd rather have a tooth removed. He didn't want to seem a big-head or a braggart, but the truth is that Errol is the World Kick-Boxing Champion, he is Steven Spielberg's personal bodyguard and, at the time, he was contracted to Warner Bros., looking after the stars on the film *Matrix*.

That's to name just a few of his accomplishments. But it hasn't always been an easy ride for Errol. His life has been a roller coaster of turbulent twists and turns. He's a complex character full of deep, dark secrets still to be uncovered. There are parts of Errol's life that he is still unable to speak about. The things that have happened to him are just too painful for words. Errol has stared adversity in the face and overcome it through sheer hard work and determination. This is the reason why he is a hard man, and the most sought-after bodyguard both in this country and America. Cross him and you'll see why.

ERROL FRANCIS

BACKGROUND

I was born in Jamaica. I was five years old when I came to England. I went to live in Goose Green, East Dulwich in London. My father was the first black man to be a manager. It was a furniture shop in Brixton called Williams. At that time, most black men were either bus or train drivers but my father was always suited and booted. He had a good job and, on the surface of it, he was a good, law-abiding citizen. But behind closed doors he was a tyrant and my worst enemy.

My dad had a saying: 'Bend a tree while it's young,' and that's what he tried to do with me. He beat me terribly.

I started going to the gym to let out some of my aggression and to get some attention. My trainer was the only man ever to say, 'Well done, Errol,' and I liked it. I started boxing and took up martial arts. At the time, Bruce Lee was popular and I'd go to late-night showings at the pictures and study his every move. At last I'd found a niche in life and the one thing I was good at – knocking people out, no argument.

I worked hard and I became the World Kick-Boxing Champion and a celebrity bodyguard. I now run the biggest club in South London and take kids off the street, training them to be British champions.

At the moment, I'm training for Mr Universe 2000. Training keeps my aggression in a safe place.

LIFE OF CRIME

Violence has always been part of my life – it's the only thing I really know. As a child growing up that's all I experienced and I thought that's what adults did – bash each other up. I went from an approved school to a detention centre and then eventually to prison. All for violent crimes, inevitably ending in murder. I served six years inside, but was sentenced to ten.

WEAPONRY

I'm a great thinker. All my fights take place in my head first. So my mind is my greatest weapon.

TOUGHEST MOMENT

I've got to say preparation for any fight. I've always found that tough. Preparing to knock out an opponent or to defend myself. To gauge how hard to hit someone so as not to kill them. Just enough to maim, break a bone, knock out or stun. I think about every move carefully and will only hit someone according to what they have done to me.

IS THERE ANYONE YOU ADMIRE?

God. There is no one higher.

DO YOU BELIEVE IN CAPITAL PUNISHMENT?

Yes, I do for child abusers.

IS PRISON A DETERRENT?

No. It's a criminal breeding ground.

WHAT WOULD HAVE DETERRED YOU FROM A LIFE OF CRIME?

Nothing.

WHAT MAKES A TOUGH GUY?

The truth and being straight. A man can't be wrong and strong. If a person is wrong, he'll try and defend himself with his mouth but in his heart he has fuck all.

ERROL'S FINAL THOUGHT

When I was growing up I really thought that violence was how people got what they wanted. I now know that is rubbish. When I first came to this country, I was five years old. I stepped off the plane from Jamaica not knowing what to expect. For the first time I saw grey skies, big red buses and kids with ginger hair and freckles. I was told to eat with a knife and fork and was forced to wear shoes. All these things were alien to me. But the one thing that is universal, no matter where you come from or what colour you are, is: if you have a pound note then you have lots of friends and if you're a nice man, people walk all over you. When you say, 'No more, man, I've had enough, I won't be beaten any more,' and retaliate, then I become the nutcase. Now I'm the bad guy.

The Bowers

I'm waiting for the Bower brothers in the lounge of the Peacock Gym, east London, when it suddenly occurs to me that I might not recognise them – which would be really embarrassing. All I know is that they're three very good-looking brothers.

I'd heard about the Bowers many times, but I'd never actually met them. I'd heard that they were this and I'd heard that they were that, but mainly I'd heard that they were a family not to mess with; if you fuck with one then you take them all on! They don't flaunt themselves in public and they don't do the hard sell on the social scene – in fact, they are very private men.

As I waited for them to arrive I looked around the gym and, in particular, at the many photos of young boxers hanging on the wall. There were numerous photographs of youngsters from the local neighbourhood whom they have encouraged and helped. Literally hundreds.

83

The Peacock Gym is the most famous gym in London because it has the best facilities for young and old.

A receptionist asked if she could be of any assistance; I said I was waiting for the Bower brothers. Then they appeared through a doorway, and I immediately experienced those penetrating, ridiculously brown brown eyes probing the room. All three of them look like Hollywood film stars from a gangster movie.

Basically, it was male testosterone at its height – untamed charisma. Their shirts matched – silk and velvet – to complement their eyes and I wondered if it was coincidence.

We moved to the patio for coffee or, in their case, weak tea. Every pair of female eyes in the room was glued to us. To put it into context, of all the people I've ever interviewed – murderers, gangsters and the hugely famous – I've never encountered such an outbreak of raw female slack-jawed lust.

The brothers took me to a palatial office on the top floor of the gym where we could talk in private. I switched on my tape recorder and placed it in between two posh desks. Tony Bowers sat behind one desk and Martin and Paul sat behind the other. They were polite and courteous throughout the interview, to me and to each other.

'Sorry, Tony, can I butt in there?' or, 'If I can just interrupt you for a moment...'

They were young men with old-fashioned values who rose to the occasion in their fine suits and silk ties embroidered with a certain dignity. They were rough diamonds. Then, with a tap on the door and a muffled 'Excuse me', in walked their father, Wally. He is the figurehead of the family and probably the only man in the world who can control the three brothers. It was at that moment I realised where the brothers had inherited their manners and dignity from.

At first, the boys were eager to tell me about the things they do for the community and were as proud as peacocks that they were a registered charity.

That wasn't what I'd come to hear; I wanted blood and guts. I wanted to know if the fearsome reputation I'd heard about them was true. But with a wave of the hand and a flash of a pearly smile, my questions were dismissed.

They didn't need to say anything; the atmosphere, the mood and the feeling that they generated between themselves was enough to send a shiver down your spine.

Reluctantly, the boys agreed to be photographed for the book and I think the image speaks for itself.

BACKGROUND

We were brought up in Canning Town, east London. We had a sister, Jayne Louise, but unfortunately she was killed.

I suppose you could say our dad Wally used to be a rascal. He's been inside a couple of times. When he was first put in prison our mum was very ill and she was always in and out of hospital so our dad's sister came to live with us. Tragically, our mum passed away. However, we still had lots of love, even though our dad was inside and Mum was no longer with us.

Us boys used to do the weekly shopping; we only had a couple of quid to do it each week but we never went short of anything. We'd put a big bag underneath the trolley and make our way round the supermarket. More things went in the bag than the trolley! We had to live by our wits, which made us strong, helped us, drove us on if you like.

As kids we didn't do much schooling, we'd rather make camps and ours was always the best around. Whenever we built our camps we'd put everything in it. Every kid in the neighbourhood wanted to come to our camp and we carried that theory on in our businesses. If you put everything into it, people will want to join you. This lesson we have taken with us through our life. But we will never forget our background; we are street urchins and always will be.

LIFE OF CRIME
Who said we had a life of crime?

WEAPONRY
Not known to use anything.

TOUGHEST MOMENT
Losing our mother and sister.

IS THERE ANYONE YOU ADMIRE?

Our father, Wally. He brought us up alone and that must have been a hard thing for a man to do in the sixties.

DO YOU BELIEVE IN CAPITAL PUNISHMENT?

No. I think that all nonces should be kept in a building. When a sick or dying patient needs a new kidney or heart, then the organs should be removed from the pervs. Don't just hang them – make use of them.

IS PRISON A DETERRENT?

No. Prison is a university and not a deterrent.

WHAT WOULD HAVE DETERRED YOU FROM A LIFE OF CRIME?

Money.

WHAT MAKES A TOUGH GUY?

A man who sticks by his family. Living by the rules. A man of his word. That's how you get respect: living by the rules.

THE BOWERS' FINAL THOUGHT

We've worked and worked for years. We've got lots of businesses – pubs, restaurants and cab firms. We've always worked. We've ducked and dived and done what we had to do to get to where we are today.

Nowadays, we try to put something back into the community instead of taking it out. We've got the biggest gym in London, The Peacock. We've got twelve football teams for children, we organise endless summer camps, amateur boxing competitions, UK Strongman, karate events, wrestling and marathons, to name but a few. It takes a lot of dedication and hard graft to keep our businesses afloat and we're lucky enough to have a good team of workers and helpers, both paid and voluntary.

Our greatest achievement is being a registered charity for the last six years. We can say hand on heart that there really is nothing like a straight pound note.

Glenn Ross

Glenn Ross punched the air in triumph, 'I'm the fucking daddy!' he yelled.

That was the first time I saw Glenn. It was at the UK Strongman contest at the Peacock Gym in east London. Other contestants were strutting around in their designer gear – Lycra shorts and skimpy vests. Glenn Ross was simply Glenn Ross. He has no time for such superficial trivia. He wore cut-down shorts and a baggy T-shirt.

There was something different about Glenn, something that set him above the rest. Not just his size, as he was, without question, the biggest man there. It was the manner in which he conducted himself. He moved casually, smiled carefully and spoke slowly.

That day, Glenn won the title of the UK's Strongest Man. The next time I saw him was on TV in The World's Strongest Man. Glenn always stuck in my mind and I knew when I started this book that I wanted to find him. I contacted the Bower brothers who own the Peacock Gym; within minutes, Glenn was on the phone and within days I was on my way to Bangor, Northern Ireland, to interview him.

As I waited for Glenn to pick me up from the airport, I couldn't have prepared myself for how he looked. I had only ever seen him in shorts and T-shirts, so when he arrived fully dressed he was double the size. In fact, I had to look twice – he was absolutely gigantic.

I made the introductions to my minder and photographer. We crossed the car park to Glenn's car. He apologised that he had his baby son Marcus with him, as he gently strapped him into the baby seat. I looked at the car. I didn't think for one moment that we would all get in. The photographer climbed in the back with the baby and I climbed in with them. My minder sat in the front. When Glenn sat in the driver's seat, the car buckled under his thirty-stone frame.

I looked at the back of his head. He hasn't got a neck, his head runs straight down to his shoulders. Everything about Glenn is big. His shoulders start underneath his ears and spread outwards like a rugged mountain. He is thirty stone of squat, solid muscle, which ripples and bulges over his collar. His hands are like Spear & Jackson shovels.

At the time I interviewed him, Glenn was sporting a black eye. I asked him how he got it; he said that he had thrown a couple of troublemakers out of a club in

Belfast and had copped one in the eye. God knows what happened to the men he threw out!

That's just it; the way Glenn looks and the way he is are the complete opposite. I noticed the purple and red scars on his bulky forearms. I imagined that they were battle scars from fending off this blow or that. But they weren't. I was amazed to learn that Glenn used to be a pastry chef. The marks on his arms were scalds from a hot oven when he put the pastry and cakes in to cook. Life is full of surprises. It only confirms that you should never judge a book by its cover.

We arrived at Bangor marina to do the interview. Everywhere we went, Glenn was recognised. People approached him and asked for an autograph or a photo for the album. Glenn is very approachable and eager to please and signed and posed with a smile. We took the photographs for the book on the dockside: then had lunch in a quaint restaurant overlooking the cold, bleak Irish Sea.

We ate Irish mussels in garlic sauce while Glenn tenderly fed his baby son scrambled egg. He clucked and cooed over his offspring like a mother hen.

He was proud as punch and didn't give a toss about trying to be macho or something that he wasn't. To me, this was like a breath of fresh air.

Glenn wants to break into the world of show business. I suggested with caution that he enrol with the London-based agency Ugly. I didn't mean it in an offensive way and Glenn didn't take it that way. He was just pleased that I wanted to help. When I got back to London, I signed him up with three agencies. When the agents for Ugly saw the photographs of Glenn, they also immediately put him on their books. Glenn was grateful for the help and chuffed to mint-balls when he got his first assignment.

He's currently training hard for the European and World's Strongest Man competition. He rubbed his hands gleefully.

'This is going to be my year. I'm going to be The World's Strongest Man 2000.' And, with a wink and a smile, he added, 'Please God!'

BACKGROUND

I am the eldest of two brothers and one sister. I weighed nine pounds when I was born and was always big as a child. My father was a sales rep. Unfortunately, I no longer speak to my mother or father – I haven't done for ten years. I won't go into the details or reasons why we fell out, but let's just say it involved my grandad. So when I got married, my grandad was the man on the top table at my reception, not my father.

Due to my dad's job, I spent a lot of my childhood in England, mainly in Warrington, Cheshire. Half my life I've been to and from Warrington and Northern Ireland. That's probably why I love travelling. I'm not a good traveller though, as the seats are never big enough!

I left school when I was sixteen to join the Boys'

Service, which is a springboard into the Army. I did three years Boys' Service and then signed up as a soldier for a further three years and trained to be a chef. It was in the Army that I first started physical training and I loved it. The Army turns you into a man but they also like to keep you a boy, with the control element, curfews and restrictions – I didn't like that. I wanted something different and left the Army at twenty-one. I took up catering full-time but continued with my training.

I won the All-Ireland Bodybuilding Championship and went on to win the UK Strongman and I haven't looked back since. In the year 2000, I aim to be the World Champion Strongman.

LIFE OF CRIME
My life has been spotlessly clean.

WEAPONRY
My greatest weapon is my size.

TOUGHEST MOMENT
My first job as a doorman was in a club called The Coach Inn, Belfast. In the past, the club had a lot of problems with drug dealers and paramilitaries. In my line of work, if I see two men fighting in the club, I chuck them out, no questions, but in Belfast, things are not that plain and simple. Two men I chucked out of the club for fighting over drugs on a Saturday night were paramilitaries and they sanctioned a punishment beating on me.

It started off with the windows in my house being smashed. I came home from work to find my car burnt out. I didn't want my family hurt, so I moved to a wee town outside Portadown, but they found out where I lived. I'd heard a whisper that something was going to happen so I had a 'piece' hidden in my car.

November 1996. I finished work late; I was tired and all I wanted to do was get home to my wife Yvonne and have my dinner. I parked my car around the corner from my house. It was dark, no one was around. I didn't want to take my 'piece' home for my wife to see so I left it in my motor.

I locked the door and took two steps from the car. As I did, eight or ten guys ran from behind a row of garages. They were wearing boiler suits and brand-new balaclavas over their faces; they were real thick wool, I could see that in the light. I just remember thinking that this was it, I'm going to get fucking shot.

I knew there was a river behind me and I thought, well, guns can't swim, if I can make it across the river then I'll be all right. All I wanted to do was lead them away from my house; if they were going to kneecap me or shoot me in the back of the head then I didn't want my wife to witness it. I made a dash for a field behind me. It was pitch-black. I ran across the field towards the river.

I could hear them chasing me. I weigh nearly thirty stone so I'm not the most athletic person in the world but I ran as fast as I could. Just before I hit the river, I fell down some kind of fucking hole, a rabbit or pothole.

As I tried to get up, I felt a blow to my head. I looked up and was surrounded by the men, holding pick-axe handles.

My first thought was, well, at least they're not going to shoot me; they're here to give me a beating. I just remember them swinging the pick-axe handles and bringing them down on my head again and again. I put my hands up to defend myself, but it was no good. The only thing I had in my defence was my size. I charged at one of them. I took a couple more blows round the head but managed to grab one of the pick-axe handles. I felt a couple more blows to my head; half-dazed, I lashed out. I swung the handle as hard as I could and brought it down on one of the attackers' heads. He screamed. I hit him again and again with all my might. I was bashing him out of sheer desperation – literally for my life. I couldn't see what I was hitting, blood was gushing down my face, but I could feel the guy on the floor. He wasn't moving. I started swinging the handle, shouting, 'Come on, come on, you bastards!'

Two guys grabbed the man on the floor and started dragging him up the hill. I turned round; three or four guys were standing behind me. I wiped the blood from my eyes and waved the handle in the air.

'Come on then. Do you want some?'

They shit themselves and ran off. It was unbelievable, absolutely unbelievable, and I'll tell you now if they had stood for another two minutes they'd have finished me because my head was literally lying open. I waved the pick-axe handle in the air, shouting, 'Come back, you yellow bastards!'

As they disappeared out of sight, I remember saying to myself, 'Shut up, Glenn.' Then I collapsed. I had sixty staples put in my head but at least I was alive.

IS THERE ANYONE YOU ADMIRE?

My grandad, because he was a war veteran. In my sport, I admire Bill Kazmaier. He won the title of The World's Strongest Man and is the strongest man on the planet. On a personal level, I admire my wife Yvonne, for giving me my son and for putting up with me.

DO YOU BELIEVE IN CAPITAL PUNISHMENT?

Yes. If anybody kills someone from the security forces, a policeman or commits more than two murders, hang them. Oh, and let's not forget rapists and child abusers. They should definitely hang.

IS PRISON A DETERRENT?

No. In Northern Ireland, a prisoner hands in his 9mm Browning handgun and they are given a mobile phone. Also, they are allowed conjugal rights with their wives and prison officers can't go onto the landings. That's no punishment or deterrent.

WHAT WOULD HAVE DETERRED YOU FROM A LIFE OF CRIME?

I haven't been in trouble with the law and have never been to prison.

WHAT MAKES A TOUGH GUY?

Somebody who has respect from others and not fear. A man who respects his family and puts them number one before all else, even before himself.

DO YOU HAVE ANY REGRETS?

Generally, I don't have any real regrets. I suppose I regret the way things have turned out with my family – my mum and dad and brothers and sister – but that's life, it's a decision I made. I am a firm believer in fighting for what you want. A man has to stand up and be counted, no matter who you are. It's better to stand tall than be small.

John
McGinnis

What you see is what you get with John McGinnis. There are no frills, no pleasantries, just John. He doesn't dress to please or to impress, he's a man who is at peace with himself.

Usually when I'm doing an interview, it's either in a gym or a hotel or club, and I was surprised when John invited me to his house to talk to him. He lives in a quaint little village on the outskirts of Kent. It's an idyllic setting, with privet hedges and rose bushes. His home has a warm, cosy feel to it; John sat in John's chair with John's mug full of hot tea. Beside him were John's slippers and John's dog. It was blatantly obvious he's a creature of habit and dislikes change. I recognised that straight away.

John told me, 'I've been doing door work for twenty-seven years. Girls are the worst, you know. When women are in drink – they're murder. I've had them attack me, gob in my face, then scream blue murder if I try to chuck 'em out.'

John is an old hand at door work. There's nothing you can tell him that he hasn't already seen. He's a master in his field. It's as comforting to him as his old worn armchair indoors.

I went to the club to see where he works. It was like a home from home. Just like in his front room, John sat in his usual spot – in John's chair, with John's newspaper and John's usual bottle of beer. He sits in the doorway reading his newspaper, barely bothering to look up at the young revellers coming into the club.

There's nothing in John's face to suggest that he is anything other than just a nice bloke. Until, that is, there's a disturbance inside the club. He reluctantly puts down his paper and beer and excuses himself. It's at that moment John's persona changes. The warm, friendly bloke disappears and out comes John's alter ego – a nasty bastard. In a flash, the look in his eyes turns to hatred. I was amazed; it was such a turnaround. It was at that point that he was transformed into all the things that I'd heard about him: powerful, fiercely aggressive and dogmatic. And that's the reason why I just had to include him in *Ultimate Hard Men*.

BACKGROUND

I was born in Woolwich, south-east London. My old man was always in and out of prison, with a criminal record dating back to 1940. He was born in Northern Ireland, which is where it all started, with minor burglaries. My dad was a wiry old fox and served twenty-one years of his life inside. He only weighed thirteen-and-a-half stone but, boy, could he have a fucking row! He was a drinker and it was the booze that killed him in the end.

He spent most of his life in England but, as with most Paddies, they all consider Ireland as home. When my dad was in hospital half-dead from the ravages of drink, all he talked of was seeing Northern Ireland just once more. He made the journey home, but never made it back; he was buried in Northern Ireland.

While at the funeral I met cousins that I didn't even know existed. They were horse traders and tinkers, Paddies through and through, just like my dad.

Up until the age of sixteen I lived in kids' homes, but it was one of my uncles that took me to work on a door. It never made me a millionaire, just paid for the groceries.

LIFE OF CRIME

I've been inside once and once was enough. I got three years for a violent attack.

WEAPONRY

I've always got a 'piece' in the back of the motor and anyone that hasn't I think is a fool. When I have a row I don't use it every time, but I know it's there – just in case.

TOUGHEST MOMENT

Call me superstitious, but I've always had a thing about door work and I've never looked after a pub or club unless I knew for certain it was going to be long term. All the places I've looked after have always been long-term contracts, including the one I'm at now. It's been seven years and Woolwich before that was thirteen. If I'm going to sort out a club and make it safe by putting my life on the line, then it's got to be a good earner for me. I've got to stamp my mark from the outset and if that means having a row then so fucking be it.

I've had lots of confrontations that can sometimes spill over as an offshoot from my door work.

I'd had a little run in on a Friday night with some 'herberts'. They were boozed up and playing up. I slung them out of the club – simple as that. Later in the evening, my friend came in and said that he'd seen them hanging around outside. He said he thought they were carrying something. I went outside to have a look and, before I knew it, I was being shot at. One of the bullets missed me by a fraction. It was a very, very dodgy night!

IS THERE ANYONE YOU ADMIRE?

People that are loyal to each other and don't grass. Oh, and anybody that gets one over on the Old Bill!

DO YOU BELIEVE IN CAPITAL PUNISHMENT?

I think that certain people deserve to be hanged. There are two kinds of murderers: if a couple of geezers are having a row in a pub and one bloke dies, that's just bad luck. Then there are people like paedophile Sidney Cook. They are the scum of the earth. I'd hang them from the nearest tree.

IS PRISON A DETERRENT?

Not when you're younger, but it is when you're older. When I did my 'bird' I was double fit and could handle it, but when you're older you've got more to lose.

The worst thing for me was when my wife came to visit me every two weeks with the kids. They were only babies and the hardest thing for me was to watch them walk out of the prison. It's such a fucking waste of time but you've just got to get on with it.

WHAT WOULD HAVE DETERRED YOU FROM A LIFE OF CRIME?

I'm not saying that I don't do things illegal, but I wouldn't do them full-time. The thing that deters me now is more 'bird'.

WHAT MAKES A TOUGH GUY?

Not getting beaten up locally. I might go on holiday to a Greek island and get a chair whacked over my head but no one knows about it. If you get stuck on your arse on your doorstep by someone, your respect and reputation flies straight out of the window. A real hard bastard is someone who can take a hiding, and give one.

JOHN'S FINAL THOUGHT

I think drugs have changed things today. It's made everyone a lot slimier. They bring out the worst in everyone. I see it every night I'm working on the door. It could be the skinniest of kids but when he's out of his head he'd think nothing of stabbing or shooting you. They think they're invincible. It's a shame but it's the way of the world today.

Bobby Wren

No one will ever get to the bottom of Bobby Wren. I can't fathom out whether he's SAS, ex-military, mercenary or just a dangerous bastard. He's an odd-bod, a loner. A modest, reserved enigma. Bobby is gadget mad and has sophisticated paraphernalia for just about everything.

I sat in Spencers pub in Hornchurch, Essex, waiting to interview Bobby – he was late. My minder ordered me another orange juice from the bar while I fiddled with my tape recorder. I glanced at my watch and thought to myself, I'll give him another five minutes. At that moment the saloon door burst open and in scurried Bobby Wren, suited and booted, carrying a holdall. He was sweating profusely and apologised for being late. I asked him if he'd been running for a bus or something. He scowled, 'I've just finished training!'

By the size of him, he wasn't kidding. His shoulders

are so broad he could carry the weight of the whole world on them.

During our interview Bobby showed me up-to-date heat-seeking equipment, bugging devices, and a gadget that he wears on his chest that vibrates if someone close to him is armed. While I was with him he wanted to demonstrate sixty ways to break a man's arm in under a minute – I declined.

Bobby is a strange, complex character who holds his cards close to his chest – probably next to the vibrating gadget!

I've known Bobby for some years but the incident about him that sticks out in my mind most happened when Ron died.

I stood by the freshly dug grave. The vicar stood at the end. 'Ashes to ashes, dust to dust...'

Something distracted me and I glanced over my shoulder. A man dressed in combat clothes, wearing a woolly hat and carrying a gun appeared from behind a gravestone. His eyes bulged and he fixed me with a steely gaze. He winked and disappeared as quickly as he had arrived – it was Bobby Wren. I later learnt that he'd staked out the graveyard three days before the funeral. I don't know what he thought was going to happen, but in a macabre way it was comforting knowing someone was watching out for me.

Bobby took a lot of persuading to be included in this book and, even when he finally agreed, he was very reluctant to talk about the things he'd been involved in. What intrigued me about him was the mysterious holdall that was his constant companion. It was a large blue canvas bag with lots of zips and compartments. It was full to bursting and Bobby is very secretive about what it contains.

From time to time during the interview, Bobby would delve into the mystery holdall and produce some gadget or other, or a bulging file containing top-secret information on this person or that. I noticed George Harrison's name on the top of one of the files. This was shortly after the attempted murder of the ex-Beatle.

I asked Bobby if it was his security company that had been assigned to look after George. Bobby paused and threw me a look, a Bobby Wren look, a look of contempt, a 'how dare you?' look. Instinctively, I knew not to pursue the matter any further.

At the end of the interview, Bobby excused himself to use the toilet. He picked up his mystery holdall and placed it precariously on the table in front of me. I wanted to have a peek inside but remembered the old saying, 'curiosity killed the cat'.

I got up from my seat and approached the bar to speak to my minder and photographer. Out of the corner of my eye, I noticed Bobby Wren standing in the doorway, furtively spying through the window at me. What was he expecting to see? Perhaps he was waiting for me to go through his holdall? I noticed the bag was positioned very carefully and remembered that he'd moved the ashtray and some empty glasses on the table to position his concealed bag of tricks. It was then I asked myself, was there a surveillance camera or bugging device in the mystery holdall? Was he testing or listening? I'll probably never know.

BACKGROUND
I was born and brought up in Crystal Palace. One of five children. That's all I'm prepared to say.

LIFE OF CRIME
I do have convictions, but I'd rather not say what they are.

WEAPONRY
My arms and legs are my deadliest weapons. I also have a section 5 firearms licence.

TOUGHEST MOMENT
Not prepared to say.

IS THERE ANYONE YOU ADMIRE?
No.

DO YOU BELIEVE IN CAPITAL PUNISHMENT?
No, 'cos there but for the grace of God go I.

IS PRISON A DETERRENT?

No. Prison is a demoralising waste of time. You leave your morals and dignity at the gate when you go in, and pick them up on the way out. But something has to be done to keep law and order.

WHAT WOULD HAVE DETERRED YOU FROM A LIFE OF CRIME?

I'm straight. What I do is in self-defence.

WHAT MAKES A TOUGH GUY?

An honest man. Someone who can hold his head up with dignity.

BOBBY'S FINAL THOUGHT

Violence is my job. It's what I do best. I'm not bragging or trying to be flash, it's just the way it is. I'm dedicated to my profession – I have to be to stay alive. I've been trained in eighteen different martial arts; I've been taught to disarm a man whilst blindfolded; I can show you sixty ways to break your arm and pressure points that can bring a man to his knees in seconds. It's hard to describe my job. It hasn't got an exact label, or title. Some say SAS. Others say mercenary.

I can't, for legal and security reasons, elaborate on the things that I've been involved in, but the dictionary definition of mercenary is a man hired to fight and kill solely for money. I guess that sums me up.

Ronnie Field

Ronnie is a man who changes his moods as swiftly as a chameleon changes its colour. He doesn't pander to whims, but is a force to be reckoned with. He demands respect. A commander of men,

Ronnie is always immaculately dressed in starched white shirts and well-cut suits. He projects an image of respectability, but cross him and he will fight like a devil.

He's currently residing in one of 'Her Majesty's big houses'. That's a polite way of saying he's banged up in the slammer – nine years for intent to supply cocaine.

I've known Ron for eleven years. He was my minder while I was married to Ronnie. There are so many stories I could tell you about Ronnie Fields. Some are funny, some are frightening and some are sinister. But I can't tell you any of these for obvious reasons. I would if I could, but I can't so I won't.

During the time I've known Ron, he's been to prison a couple of times; he never complains or makes a song and dance about being sent down. It's just a hazard of his profession – armed robbery. But the sentence he's serving at the moment is different. I know for a fact that Ron is not a drug baron, never has been and never will be. It's just not his bag. The way he was treated stinks! It should be illegal.

BACKGROUND

I was born in Epsom, Surrey, the youngest of seven children. My father was a safe-blower who learnt his trade in the Army. He was a highly decorated soldier at the D-Day landings and crossing of the Rhine. Dad left home when I was four years old. Me and my brothers were left with my grandmother – she was a tyrant. I was lucky she left me alone.

LIFE OF CRIME

1976 – I was sentenced to twelve years for an armed robbery on a wages office in Leeds. I got another ten years for an armed robbery on a supermarket in Wimbledon. In 1991, I was arrested at Gatwick airport for conspiracy to commit armed robbery – estimated value, ten million pounds. I was sentenced to five years for that one!

1996 – Me, Charlie Kray and one other were arrested by undercover police for supplying cocaine. I received nine years, Charlie Kray received twelve, the other mate five years. I'm guilty of the other armed robberies; I'll put my hands up to those, it was a fair cop! But for supplying cocaine, I know the truth. The whole thing stank from start to finish. The fucking thing felt like entrapment, which is no defence in this country, although it is in every other European state.

I'll do the nine years standing on my head, but it's wrong, plain and simple. I'm not saying this because I'm trying to get out of my sentence, because I've nearly completed it. I'm saying it because it is wrong. There's a word which means 'to catch or snare in a trap', and that's just what happened to me, Charlie Kray and a mate.

WEAPONRY
See no evil, hear no evil, speak no evil.

TOUGHEST MOMENT
My toughest moment was when my mother died and I didn't get a chance to say sorry for all the worry I'd given her. Also, the day my baby daughter died was probably my darkest hour.

IS THERE ANYONE YOU ADMIRE?
I don't know if 'admire' is the right word, but probably the only man I'd trust with my life is Joey Pyle. He is a man of honour and one I respect.

DO YOU BELIEVE IN CAPITAL PUNISHMENT?

Yes, for sex offenders and killers of children. There is no cure and they never change, despite what doctors and do-gooders say. In prison the nonces and ponces are mollycoddled as if they are sick. They're sick all right – sick in the fucking head. They don't need help, they need stringing up.

IS PRISON A DETERRENT?

I suppose prison is a deterrent to a certain extent. Nobody wants to go to prison and the older you get, the more of a deterrent it becomes.

WHAT WOULD HAVE DETERRED YOU FROM A LIFE OF CRIME?

Dough, loot, moolah, lolly, spondoolies – what else?

WHAT MAKES A TOUGH GUY?

A man who shouts from the rooftops telling everyone that he's bashed this one and bashed that one or killed this one and killed that one – he is nothing but a fool. It's the quiet, unobtrusive man that is dangerous.

RONNIE'S FINAL THOUGHT

I should have sussed it. I should have sussed his boots – black, polished Dr. Martens.

To tell the truth, I had been clean for a while; I never intended to do any more 'work'. I wanted to spend some quality time with my daughter Sadie and my grandson and just have a rest. I didn't want any more 'cozzers' kicking my door open in the middle of the night. I'm not saying that I was ready for pipe and slippers, but I wanted to take a back seat – at least for a while.

From time to time I'm asked to go to 'work' with this one or that. Usually, I stick to my own, never venturing away from the people I know and trust. Then, out of the blue, I got a call from someone I knew, but wasn't a friend. He explained about a job that he was involved in. It sounded good – fucking good. He offered me a bit of the action and I've got to admit I was tempted. Foolishly, I decided to meet the men offering the 'bit of work'. Well, it couldn't hurt just meeting them.

Arrangements were made to meet in a quiet pub on the outskirts of London. The pub was unfamiliar to me – it was out of my manor. I should have just turned round and walked away, but I didn't. Instead, I ordered a round of drinks and listened. I said nothing, just listened. From the outset, I didn't like the set-up. I had a gut feeling, something just wasn't right. I felt a bit uncomfortable, but pushed it to the back of my mind.

There was talk of kilos and kilos of cocaine. Ten million pounds, fifteen million pounds, twenty-two million pounds' worth of charlie. It was rootin', tootin' big-time and not my scene. I told 'em to count me out. But the boys were nothing if not persistent.

All sorts of outlandish figures were bandied around.

I'm not a mug, I've been up to skulduggery for as long as I can remember. I'm not sure if the boys persuaded me or I convinced myself that the job was a good idea. The more I listened, the more I began to wobble.

'How easy? How much?'

I thought to myself that if I did this one, the big 'un, then I could settle down and behave myself – for good!

I asked my mate how well he knew the other blokes. With a wave of his hand, he dismissed the question, 'Oh, I've known them for years. They're kosher …'

I looked at their tanned faces and false smiles. The Armani suits. The Rolex watches. The flash cars. They had all the trappings. It was at that point I noticed their boots. I asked suspiciously, 'You ain't Old Bill, are ya?'

They were cool. Inside, they must have been dying. I should have gone with my gut feeling and got my sorry arse out of there. I didn't.

If I can pass on anything from my experiences to a young, up-and-coming villain, it's this: always judge a man by his shoes. If he wears worn, black, polished Dr. Marten boots, then tell him in no uncertain terms to 'fuck off'. Because make no mistake – he's Old Bill.

Stellakis Stylianou

Stilks' physique is that of an athlete, he's wiry and fast. In his line of work, speed is of the essence – and I don't mean a 'dab' of the white powder. He has to be able to defuse situations before they erupt into violence. The difference between him and most other meaty doormen is experience. I hate to quote a corny cliché, but he has been there, done it, and got every fucking T-shirt available.

I asked Stilks whether perhaps he thrived on dangerous situations and did he ever get nervous.

'Nah, I don't get nervous. I wasn't even worried when a gang was going to lynch me for refusing them entry to a club. It's just part and parcel of security work.'

I studied his rugged face. His strong features gave nothing away. He has a prominent nose and beady eyes and gives the impression that he is almost bomb-proof. I interviewed him at his home in Sidcup on the outskirts of London. As I knocked on the front door, I noticed that one of the windows was broken. Once inside, I asked his pretty wife Sheena how it was broken. She tutted and sighed, 'It's 'im. He forgot his keys again.'

She went on to tell me that Stilks is forgetful. 'It's his age,' she teased.

'I'm not old.' He winked. 'I can still chase ya round the kitchen and catch ya!' They looked at each other and laughed, sharing a private joke.

They were obviously a couple who were comfortable with each other and still very much in love after twenty-four years of marriage. Stilks waited until his wife left the room, then whispered, 'She's pregnant again, ya know. I've got four daughters, maybe this time we'll have a boy, then I'll retire from working on the doors. But don't mention it to Sheena... Shh, she's coming back ...'

Stilks was like a naughty boy. The cat that ate the cream. Sheena put the tea down on the polished coffee table and smiled a radiant smile. Stilks puffed his chest out with pride. They were a smashing couple.

I was glad Stilks was considering retiring from door work. It was a nice thought and an even nicer thing to say to his pregnant wife. But I think the promise may have been made in haste, maybe in the flush of pride of an expectant father.

I really think the word retirement is not applicable to men like Stilks; it's more suited to bank managers and accountants. When you've been a tough guy all your life, you can't just give it up, it's not that simple, because you can never retire from what and who you really are...

BACKGROUND

I was born in Plumstead, south London. Although I was born in England, I couldn't speak English until I was seven. My parents were from Cyprus. Mum and Dad tried to be strict with me, but by the age of fourteen I'd become uncontrollable. Then I started going to a local youth club and was introduced to judo – I loved it. It was a way of expressing myself in a positive rather than negative way. It became a way of life and I enjoyed it for twelve years. Each level and each belt I won gave me great satisfaction and when I won my black belt by beating a line-up of six opponents one after the other, it was the pièce de résistance!

LIFE OF CRIME

Nothing to speak of.

WEAPONRY

I've hit a few people with chairs but I never carry a knife or a knuckle-duster because I think, on the spur of the moment, I'd use it. I've broken my hand five times where I've hit people on the head. So I find the quickest and easiest way to control a violent situation is to use strangulation.

TOUGHEST MOMENT

It was late August and the football season had just started. I was working on a door at a hotel. Millwall supporters were celebrating a win. They were full of lager and up for a row. I was having none of it and told them to leave. There was a bit of a scuffle but I got them out and thought no more of it.

At the end of the night, as usual, I was hungry and fancied a kebab. I told the boys to start locking up and that I wouldn't be long. I made my way down a dimly lit road towards the late-night take-away. Call it a gut feeling or instinct, but I felt I was being followed. I couldn't quite put my finger on it, but something didn't feel right.

Halfway down the road I heard footsteps behind me. I glanced over my shoulder and saw four blokes running towards me with sticks. I recognised them as the men I'd thrown out of the club earlier.

In my panic I looked around but there was no one in sight. I had no alternative but to run towards my attackers. I grabbed the stick off the first bloke and bashed him round the head with it and he fell to the floor. I thought, If I'm going to get done, I'm taking this one with me. I pushed my fingers into his eyes and he screamed in agony. The others started beating me over the head and back, but I didn't care. All I focused on was keeping a firm grip on the one I had on the floor. He was screaming like a stuffed pig.

In a situation like that you don't really feel pain; the adrenalin blocks it out. I was taking blows from every angle. I was hit on the left side of my head, then the right, I saw stars and for a moment I thought I was going to pass out. But I held on – I had to. I just remember car headlights, people screaming and noise – then nothing. I thought I was dead.

IS THERE ANYONE YOU ADMIRE?

A man called Johnny Madden. He was head doorman at the Camden Palace and also at the Hippodrome. Johnny Madden is a man of respect and a man of principle. He gently eased me into door work and told me the dos and don'ts. That was twenty-three years ago and we've remained friends ever since.

DO YOU BELIEVE IN CAPITAL PUNISHMENT?

Yes. For paedophiles and serial rapists. Not forgetting the serial killers. String 'em up! That's all they deserve.

IS PRISON A DETERRENT?

Yes, for some. On one hand I've got a friend, a good friend, who's a big, strong and well-respected man. I worked with him on the doors for ten years. He was a brave, fearless man, who wasn't frightened to take risks. He was sentenced to nine months in prison and he did six, but he couldn't muck it. When he came out of prison, he didn't leave his house for a year. I've asked him many times to come back on the door, but he refuses. He got himself a little nine-to-five job and became 'normal'. So, yes, it deterred him.

On the other hand, I've got friends who've done five, ten, fifteen years and they're still active. It didn't deter them. So it depends on the make-up of the individual.

WHAT WOULD HAVE DETERRED YOU FROM A LIFE OF CRIME?

If I thought that I would not be able to see my wife and kids for a long period of time, then that would deter me. In saying that, when you're up to no good, you don't think you're going to get caught.

WHAT MAKES A TOUGH GUY?

If I hit a man and knock him down and he jumps to his feet and comes back at me, then I knock him down for the second time and he still won't give in – is he a hard bastard or a stupid one? In my eyes, he has no fear, which makes him a tough guy.

STILKS' FINAL THOUGHT

I've done door work for twenty-three years and in that time I've had to deal with many confrontations in which I've felt my life was being threatened. I've been attacked by people you'd never dream in a million years would attack you. When I was first on the door I was gullible and I'd give people the benefit of the doubt.

One cold Saturday night I stood on the door with my hands deep in my overcoat pockets. A customer tried to get into the club and I noticed he was wearing jeans, so I refused him entry.

'Is it all right if I wait here?' he asked, shivering in the doorway.

I shrugged. 'If you like.'

For the next ten minutes I saw people in and out of the club. Suddenly, with no warning, the man standing in the doorway hit me over the back of the head and ran up the road.

I was stunned. I leant against the wall for a moment to gather my thoughts. This was lesson number one: when you tell someone to go, they go. There are no exceptions.

I hold the dubious record for being the longest-serving doorman. During my time as a doorman I've been hit, punched and shot at. The lesson I learnt is: never underestimate anyone, no matter how big or small.

Johnny
Frankham

'Whatever you do, don't mention his ear!'

I looked at Johnny Frankham, he looked at me; his face dead-pan. As we approached his brother Sam, I noticed that half his ear was missing. There was a group of travelling boys all around us. Again, he whispered, 'Whatever you do, don't mention his ear.'

Sam approached me with an outstretched hand. I shook his hand and smiled. Automatically, my eyes were drawn to his ear – if you can call it an ear. It looked more like a pig's corkscrew tail.

'There,' Johnny said, 'you looked at it ... you looked at his ear, didn't you?'

I wasn't sure if he was joking or serious.

I smirked. 'I didn't, I didn't look.'

Johnny's face gave nothing away, he was adamant.

'Yes you did. You looked at his ear, I saw you, and so did Sam.'

For a moment there was a silence. All the travelling boys looked at me; I looked at Johnny, his rugged face expressionless. Phil – the man who'd brought me to the campsite and was responsible for my safety – stood nearby. I glanced at him for something, I don't really know what, reassurance maybe. Phil winked. Only then I knew that Johnny was pulling my leg. The gypsy boys erupted into coarse, raucous laughter and I heaved a sigh of relief.

I'd gone to Berkshire to meet Johnny Frankham and his brother Sammy, King of the Gypsies. I wasn't really sure what to expect. We all have preconceived ideas of what gypsies look and live like and I was expecting to see grubby-looking men standing around bonfires with wild, untamed horses tied to a stake in a muddy field. There would probably be small children with dirty faces and snotty noses running around, swearing and spitting.

As we approached the campsite it was snowing; a thick layer of snow covered the trailers. Nobody was around, just a skinny dog tied to a kennel on a long piece of threadbare rope, barking his head off.

Phil climbed out of his Mercedes and called out to a dark-skinned lady standing in her doorway,

'Where's Johnny at?'

She pointed. 'Down the end, last trailer on the right.'

I looked around; brand-new Mercedes cars were

parked outside spanking-new mobile homes. Each was surrounded by white picket fences and neatly-kept gardens. I was shocked – it was not at all what I had expected. I was apprehensive; after all, we were strangers to the campsite. Everyone wanted to know who we were and, more importantly, what we were doing there. Net curtains twitched; suspicion filled the air as we crunched our way through the snow towards the end trailer.

Waiting for us was a tall, good-looking man, immaculately dressed. Phil made the introduction: 'This is Johnny Frankham.'

'Come in,' he said.

I walked into Johnny Frankham's home. I bent to take my shoes off, but Johnny shook his head. I stepped into the kitchen and the smell of Sunday roast was delicious. A small, pretty lady wearing a pinny and big gold earrings smiled.

'Cup of tea, luv?' she asked.

Her kitchen cabinets were full to bursting with Crown Derby china. She handed me a bone-china cup and saucer full of steaming hot tea, which I drank with caution. I wasn't used to drinking tea from such fine china.

I was shown into the lounge and stepped onto white thick-pile carpet which wouldn't have looked out of place at The Dorchester. The room was magnificent; all-white curtains with swags and tails, embroidered with gold sashes, white leather sofas and gold-edged mirrors.

Before Johnny agreed to be in the book, I had to explain in detail exactly what the book was about. After much careful thought on his part, and a little gentle persuasion on mine, he gave in.

We left the others sitting in the lounge, went into the dining room and sat at a beautiful table with a huge bowl of fresh fruit set in the middle of it.

I turned on my tape recorder and Johnny started to talk. He was a very quiet, unassuming man, not boastful in the slightest. In fact, I found him to be extremely modest, but there was something in his eyes – just something.

After the interview, he took me by the hand and showed me into a small room where his grandchildren were playing. On the wall were photographs of Johnny at the height of his boxing career. There was one photograph that caught my eye, in which Johnny stood over a man lying on the canvas. I asked him about it. He laughed.

'That's Muhammad Ali. I used to be his sparring partner when he was known as Cassius Clay.'

I was shocked – Muhammad Ali! Was this just another one of his wind-ups? But it was no joke. I read through the newspaper cuttings shaking my head in disbelief, but there it was in black and white – Cassius Clay lying on the floor in front of Johnny Frankham. It was unbelievable, there I was in a trailer in the middle of the Berkshire countryside with the man who'd knocked the greatest boxer that had ever lived to the ground. No wonder Johnny Frankham has such a fearsome reputation.

But Johnny being Johnny, he just shrugged. He wouldn't say whether it was a lucky punch, whether he hit him or whether he didn't. He just left it to my own speculation.

'Come on,' he said. 'Come and meet my brother Sam – but whatever you do, don't mention his ear …'

BACKGROUND

I was born in a tent in a field. My family have travelled all over the country. I don't come from a big family. I've got two brothers and a sister. From the age of six we toured gypsy camps going hop- or fruit-picking, depending on the season. It's natural for travelling boys to fight, but when we were kids it was never done for money. As you grow up as a gypsy, things change and it becomes more competitive.

I started amateur boxing when I was fourteen. I went through my amateur career and won all the ABAs. In between, I'd have fights with other travellers and various others who wanted to have a go. I met some tough ones, too. My brother Sam and I were the first travelling boys to start proper training and go legit. People thought we were a pushover. But me and Sam would always end up thrashing our opponents. I've got to say, I enjoyed boxing. I wasn't bad at it either.

LIFE OF CRIME

I've been in every prison in the country, but I'd rather not say why.

WEAPONRY

I've always fought with my fists, but I've kicked a few people and nutted a few people. It's part of the game.

TOUGHEST MOMENT

It was tough when I fought my brother Sam because we were friends as well as brothers. We fell out loads of times, but the first time I had to fight him was hard. He's a tough man, but at the time I was more educated than him and I'd done more training, so I beat him.

IS THERE ANYONE YOU ADMIRE?

I admire any man who'll stand up and have a fight and won't back down.

DO YOU BELIEVE IN CAPITAL PUNISHMENT?

Yes, for paedophiles and perverts.

IS PRISON A DETERRENT?

No. Prison is a stepping stone for people who want to commit crime. They learn more about crime and drugs in prison than they do outside.

WHAT WOULD HAVE DETERRED YOU FROM A LIFE OF CRIME?

Money is the only thing that would have deterred me. Crime is all down to money. All the times I've been in trouble were down to a pound note.

WHAT MAKES A TOUGH GUY?

The way you are brought up affects the way you are. If you're brought up tough then you're bound to be tough. You can't take someone out of an office and make him tough. It's all down to upbringing.

I'd rather fight someone that I knew could have a fight than someone who's a coward. You haven't got to be afraid of a man who'll fight you, but the man that's afraid could shoot you.

JOHNNY'S FINAL THOUGHT

I've had fights all over the place – fairgrounds, racetracks, fields and clubs. I know from experience that if there's a gang, it's going to be a hard fight. A man will keep fighting in front of his mates until he drops. I've banged heads, I've punched them, I've kicked them and they've still got up just because the crowd's egging them on. When the crowd's not there they just take the beating. I've been stabbed and I've been shot, but I have no regrets. Whatever I've done to another man, I've done because he deserved it.

Albert
Reading

Look up the word 'gangster' and the definition will read 'Albert Reading'. Albert is a mine of information and knows everyone there is to know, from as far away as Scotland and Liverpool. If you want anything, need anything or even need to speak to anyone, then Albert's your man.

He's infamously known as 'Boom Boom Reading'. I asked him how he got his nickname. Was it because he was known to use both gun barrels? Or was it because he was formerly a bare-knuckle fighter with punches like bombs? Albert threw his head back and laughed noisily. It wasn't any of those things. He's known as Boom Boom because he's as sly as a fox, and the puppet Basil Brush was a fox whose catchphrase was 'boom boom'.

Unlike most gangsters, Albert Reading has got a sense of humour. Maybe it's because he's a Gemini and all Geminis have a split personality. In ancient days Gemini was symbolised by twin children – Castor and Pollux of Roman mythology. A split personality is a typical Gemini trait and Albert is a typical Gemini.

On one side of the coin he is nice, good with people and sociable, the life and soul of the party, a perfect host. On the other, he's ruthless, unpredictable and can be 'fucking 'orrible' when he wants! He's a dinosaur, an old-fashioned gangster with old-fashioned ways and morals. A dying breed.

In the year 2000, Albert turned sixty-eight years old, but to him age is just a number. It hasn't slowed him down in any way, shape or form. Recently, he was given a Motability car to help him to get around. Just a normal, run-of-the-mill thing. Hundreds of people, for whatever reason, are given Motability cars and to the majority it is a big help. But Albert being Albert loaned his car to a friend – a friend who did an armed robbery in it. A Motability car on an armed robbery – some fucking friend!

'Fucking liberty,' Albert hissed. 'It was a mug-off collecting my Motability car from the police pound and even more of a mug-off that Motability took the car back!'

To Albert, the Motability saga was just an inconvenience. To him, it was nothing out of the ordinary, he took it all in his stride. How the fuck can anyone lose a Motability car in an armed robbery? It could only happen to Albert Reading.

ALBERT READING

BACKGROUND

I was born in West Ham, London, one of eight children. My father Joe was the lightweight boxer who fought under his mother's maiden name of Riley. He had over two hundred fights in his long boxing career. Unfortunately, he never kept his punches in the boxing ring and he beat me like a man throughout my young life. I've got three other brothers: Charlie, Joey and, in particular, Bobby, who became a well-respected and feared man, owing to our father's misguided belief that if he treated them rough, they'd grow up tough.

LIFE OF CRIME

My first taste of prison was in 1944; my crime was stealing a bucket of potatoes. When my father was informed, he washed his hands of me and told the authorities to let me rot to teach the little bastard a lesson. I was taken to Standard House remand home in south London. I hated the home and, two weeks later, I beat the night watchman with a billiard cue and escaped.

When I was captured, I was sent to Wormwood Scrubs, which was one of the toughest prisons in the country. I was twelve years old, the youngest person ever to be sent to the Scrubs.

Inside, I soon learnt the jargon and the pecking order and, more importantly, who the 'Daddies' were. It seemed every inmate wanted a bit of me. If they didn't want to take my belongings, they wanted to take my body. I fought tooth and nail just to survive. Constantly in trouble, I was birched three times across the arse and was unable to sit down for a week.

I served six years for stealing a bucket of potatoes. When I was released back into unsuspecting society at the age of eighteen, I was full of hate and anger. Unable to channel my aggression, I became as tough and as fearless as a wild animal, ready to wreak havoc on those who stood in my way.

For the next eight years, I stamped my mark on the underworld. Then, in 1958, I committed my first armed robbery. I'd become uncontrollable, a maniac, public enemy number one and was hunted by police all over the country. My robberies became more and more violent.

By 1960, Scotland Yard caught me and I was sentenced to twenty-five years in prison. In all, I've spent more than three decades behind bars.

WEAPONRY

I'm known to use my fists or anything to hand – a piece of wood or iron bar – but I prefer to inflict the most excruciating pain by burning my victims with acid, literally, to melt their flesh. Nothing is taboo in my eyes, but I'm not into cutting. Violence works both ways.

I've been beaten half to death by a gang, almost cut in half by another and shot in the leg and shoulder. My whole life has been a catalogue of violent incidents, but I have no qualms or regrets about the pain I've dealt out or received. To me it's just swings and roundabouts.

TOUGHEST MOMENT

I've stood toe to toe with the elite of the underworld; I've fought and beat tough men like Charlie Richardson and Mad Frankie Fraser, but one of the toughest men I ever fought was the legendary Brian Hall, formerly Henry Cooper's sparring partner and some would say the greatest bare-knuckle fighter ever.

I stepped into the ring with Hall at the age of forty-eight. Two rounds went my way; I broke Hall's nose and ribs, but in the third round he came back and beat me to the ground with cool, controlled ferocity. Still I wouldn't give in. Eventually, my corner dragged me out of the ring to save my life. The fight was one of the bloodiest this century.

IS THERE ANYONE YOU ADMIRE?

My sister Joanie, who died of a terminal illness. Just a few weeks before she died, I held her in my arms and she cried. She said she was frightened of dying. It broke my heart; I had no words of comfort. Nothing. I felt so helpless, all I could do was hold her. She was so brave, the bravest person I've ever met.

DO YOU BELIEVE IN CAPITAL PUNISHMENT?

No. I was inside when hanging was still legal. I saw innocent men go to the gallows – a man called James Hanratty and another, Flossie Forsyth.

IS PRISON A DETERRENT?

No. Prison makes you harder, shrewder and more cunning.

WHAT WOULD HAVE DETERRED YOU FROM
A LIFE OF CRIME?

The war. If there hadn't been any blackouts, then I wouldn't have started robbing.

WHAT MAKES A TOUGH GUY?

Heart. I've seen hard men hit someone, but if they don't go over with the first punch then their heart goes.

ALBERT'S FINAL THOUGHT

I always wanted to be a gangster. When I was ten years old, I nicked my dad's clothing coupons and exchanged them on the black market for a white pin-striped suit and a slug gun, just in case of trouble. It must have been an omen. When the suit fitted me that day, I knew I'd be the gangster I'd only ever dreamt of being.

All my life I've had to fight. It's been second nature. I don't know any different. I put that down to my father; he beat me mercilessly and turned me into a man when I was only a boy. The one thing he taught me, which I'm thankful for, was respect. It's a sad world when old ladies are mugged and children are abducted by paedophiles and abused. Cowards and bullies, that's all they are, preying on the old and vulnerable. Liberty-takers. I'll kill any man who tries to take a liberty with me or my family. That's not me being flash or talking big. Talk's cheap. I believe right is might.

The Bible reads: 'An eye for an eye and a tooth for a tooth.' Take a liberty with me and I'll rip both your eyes out and all your teeth. I'll beat you with my fist and an iron bar, burn you with acid or shoot you down like a dog because I can be wicked, but only if I have to be.

Carlton
Leach

I'd heard of Carlton Leach – who hasn't? He has a reputation. A reputation as a hard man. A very hard man. And he had a history.

Who hasn't heard of the Range Rover murders? Three men found dead, blasted to eternity with a shotgun, in their Range Rover, which was parked at the end of a lonely country lane in Essex. Some drug deal was supposed to be going down but it ended in blood, death and a lot of tears. One of the men, Tony Tucker, was Carlton's best friend. Carlton was his minder. For one reason or another, he hadn't been with him on that fateful night – if he had been, he would have got it too. Understandably, Carlton was devastated by Tony's death.

The first time I met Carlton, I really didn't know what to expect. When he walked into TFI Fridays on a wet Wednesday afternoon, I found that he was a good-looking man, despite all the knocks and bumps on his face, but there is a terrible sadness in his eyes.

In my opinion, what happened to Tony has been the biggest blow in his life. Carlton and Tony were mates, 'old muckers', and used to be together 24/7. That particular day, Carlton didn't go with Tony and I don't think Carlton has ever got over losing him. He's probably churned it over in his mind again and again, asking, Why? Why wasn't I with him when he needed me? In a way he blames himself, I think, and that's what you can see in his eyes.

Carlton carried Tony's coffin at the funeral and, when we were filming *Hard Bastards* for Channel 5, we took him to that lane and he became very emotional. By a strange coincidence, it was the anniversary of the killings.

He said he felt Tony all around him. At times he stumbled over his words and clearly found it hard to go on. He did cry. Real tears and lots of them. Suddenly he said he didn't want to do the TV show – it was just too painful. Still, after the initial shock of being in that lonely lane subsided, Carlton recovered. He was apologetic, crazy and funny and quite easy-going. We must have looked a picture. He's so big, we were like Little and Large.

Later, he said that he felt going there helped him release all that anger and pain. He said it was as if he was being exorcised.

One thing he couldn't do was bullshit me. When

we were filming, he tried to tell me that he didn't take steroids.

'Not that old chestnut!' I said and laughed. Then he said he only took drugs to keep him awake.

'Yeah, and I'm the Queen Mother!' I said. And then we talked. He admitted he'd taken the lot, rooted and tooted big-time – and steroids were the most terrifying. They'd turned him into a monster, a man who'd snap in a minute and use violence at the drop of a hat, a kind of Jekyll and Hyde person who could change from one to the other frighteningly fast.

The drugs had made him totally paranoid; he thought even his friends were against him, and he'd seriously thought about suicide. But Carlton is so strong he'd got through it – at least, he's getting through it. These days he keeps a low profile, preferring to cook for his friends at home rather than going out. He has a girlfriend and life seems a little slower, calmer. But the paranoia hasn't left him – he's bought a flat which is on the third floor of a building at the end of a long cul-de-sac so he can see who's coming. That gives him time to get ready – just in case.

The past still haunts him and probably always will, but maybe that's what I found amazing about him. He's been through so much. He's lived life in the fast lane, he's been stabbed and shot at, he's been through the drugs nightmare, his best friend had his head blown off. Carlton told me that, at his lowest moment, he sat in the box room of his mum's house with his hands in his head, in total despair, just wanting to die. But he's pulled himself through all that and he's getting on with his life, he's moving on. He's changed his life. He stared death in the face and spat in its eye. He said to me that he's a good boy now, a changed man, clean from drugs and crime. He told me, 'There's nothing like a straight pound note.'

Well, straight-ish ...

BACKGROUND

I was brought up in the East End, the Forest Gate/ Stratford area. My parents were out working much of the time so I had to take care of myself. There were lots of fights at school and outside. You had to learn to use your fists to earn respect and survive. I didn't like school but my dad was adamant that I should learn a trade. That way, he said, I'd always be able to find work. So, I started an apprenticeship in Engineering and Shipbuilding. As it turned out, Dad was right – after I left school, I was never out of work. But outside school and work, football was my life. West Ham. The best.

I got involved with a gang which soon became known as the notorious ICF. We'd meet up on Friday evenings in the pub and make arrangements for the following day's match. We planned it like we were going to war. And sometimes that's just what it felt like. It was a war of sorts. I have to admit that I loved the violence. The bloodier the better. It gave me that adrenalin buzz. Nothing like it. Eventually, it all changed.

Football hooliganism became a political thing. There were surveillance cameras everywhere and anyone who was suspected of causing trouble got banged up. Before, you'd just get a slapped wrist or a fine.

I started door work when I was twenty. I worked some rough clubs and learnt a lot. Then I moved on to bigger and bigger clubs until, eventually, I went into partnership with my friend Tony Tucker and we started a security firm. I was Head of Security at Ministry of Sound for a while, but we'd do security for anyone, anything. We were good. But there was a lot of drugs about and I took the lot – speed, ecstasy, coke, steroids.

The steroids made me feel invincible. But they had a bad effect on me long-term. You think you can handle it easily, but your body can't. Tony and I became involved in dealing – we provided the muscle when deals were going down. And that was the end of it. Tony and two associates of mine were blasted with a shotgun in a Range Rover in a field in Essex. I should have been there, too, but I was on an attempted murder charge at the time and couldn't risk it. So I survived – even so, that was the end of it for me.

LIFE OF CRIME

I've been nicked, arrested for violence, grievous bodily harm and for possession of Class A drugs with intent to supply, but I've never been inside. Touch wood!

IS PRISON A DETERRENT?

Yes. I spent so much of my time when I was younger on visits to people I cared for who were inside. Yes, it's a deterrent for me.

DO YOU BELIEVE IN CAPITAL PUNISHMENT?

Yes, for the right reasons. For anything where they've hurt children – I think they should be castrated or killed. Slowly.

WHAT WOULD HAVE DETERRED YOU FROM A LIFE OF CRIME?

I really don't know. Nothing really.

HAVE YOU EVER BEEN STABBED/SHOT?

I've been shot at, stabbed, glassed – oh, and I've had an axe in my head.

SCARIEST MOMENT?

I remember it well. I was on the door of a London club and I refused somebody entry. Later that evening, they came back with a gun. I couldn't – I wouldn't – run. I stood on the spot. I knew from the way he was holding the gun he wasn't joking, but I shouted at him, 'Fucking kill me!' He tried and the gun failed. That was a scary moment. Very.

SADDEST MOMENT?

My saddest day was when Tony Tucker was shot in the head. It was the saddest day of my life.

He was the other half of me. He was my brother. It's so true that when someone that close to you dies, you feel like a part of yourself has died, it's gone, it's so painful.

WHAT RATTLES YOUR CAGE?

Imposters. I hate people who pretend to be what they're not. Plastic gangsters basically – they rattle my cage.

HAVE YOU EVER REALLY LOVED ANYONE?

My children. I really love them. And Tony Tucker. He was my friend and I idolised him as I was growing up.

WHAT FRIGHTENS YOU?

Me, myself, I.

DESCRIBE A HARD BASTARD

Someone who can stand there without weapons, without tools, and still win a fight. Someone like a boxer.

NAME A HARD BASTARD

Vic Dark.

WHERE DO YOU SEE YOURSELF IN FIVE YEARS?

Hopefully alive.

ANY REGRETS?

Sometimes I have trusted the wrong people. Funnily, I don't regret my past. I've done some wicked bad things, but you can't regret your past. My past has made me the person I am today. I wish I could change some things ... but regrets? Nah.

Tony
Lambrianou

Tony Lambrianou deserves respect. He stood beside Ronnie Kray in the dock at the Old Bailey in 1968, then he did fifteen years for his part in disposing of Jack The Hat's body. He could have got a lesser sentence if he'd grassed on the twins, but he didn't. He kept his mouth shut, he did his time in some of Britain's toughest prisons and he did it like a man. For that alone, in my eyes, he deserves respect – big time.

I first met Tony on the day I married Ron. He wasn't in Broadmoor with us for the actual ceremony, but he joined the gangster party we gave for two hundred afterwards at a nearby hotel.

Tony looked – and still looks – just like you'd think a gangster should look, very Al Capone. He wouldn't look out of place in any of those old gangster movies. He was a good-looking man when he was younger. He's still a looker, but I think he has a sad face. He loves socialising and he's very much the perfect host, but perhaps what you see isn't what you get with Tony.

He has an amazing voice. The first thing that strikes you is this booming, deep, gravelly voice. If Tony says, 'Sit,' every dog in the room does – and not just the furry kind!

He's not a whinger, but I don't think Tony has had an easy time of it. It must have been very difficult for him when he came out after fifteen years with his name and reputation. He could hardly get a job serving behind the counter in the local post office, could he?

Instead, he's done the next best thing – he writes books, gives talks on the circuit about his past, his life, people he's known. A lot of people criticise him for doing that but, to me, he's got every right to do it. He lost fifteen years of his life and where does a man like him go from there?

BACKGROUND

I would rather not talk about my background. That is private, and I'd like to keep it that way.

LIFE OF CRIME

I've spent fifteen years in prison.

IS PRISON A DETERRENT?

No. There's no benefit in it, nothing at the end of it. It just doesn't do any good.

DO YOU BELIEVE IN CAPITAL PUNISHMENT?

No, they've got it wrong too many times. The last ten people they hanged – they were all dodgy cases.

WHAT WOULD HAVE DETERRED YOU FROM A LIFE OF CRIME?

Nothing. Situation and circumstance made my life what it is.

HAVE YOU EVER BEEN STABBED/SHOT?

I've been shot at twice – a couple of people have taken pot shots. But I'm still here.

SCARIEST MOMENT?

Standing in the dock and being sentenced to fifteen years. I was gutted. I looked at the future and I didn't like what I saw.

WHAT RATTLES YOUR CAGE?

False people, people who pretend to be something they're not.

HAVE YOU EVER REALLY LOVED ANYONE?

I think you can love anyone. I've loved other men as brothers, people like Ronnie and Reggie, Freddie

Foreman, friends. I loved my parents very much, my first wife and my kids – not forgetting my lady now, Wendy. I love her.

WHAT FRIGHTENS YOU?

I'm a bit long in the tooth to be frightened... Death, maybe. But we've all got to die sometime. So, nah ... I'm not frightened of anything.

DESCRIBE A HARD BASTARD

A man who stands by his principles, no matter what.

NAME A HARD BASTARD

Roy Shaw. A man would have to be brave or mad to take on Roy Shaw, the best bare-knuckle fighter in this country.

WHERE DO YOU SEE YOURSELF IN FIVE YEARS?

Hopefully, just where I am now, enjoying my life. I'm happy where I am now.

ANY REGRETS?

You can't regret anything you've done; it's gone and that's that.

Gaffer

'Fuck off! Fuck off! Fuck off!'

The manager in TGI Fridays was stunned and a look of fear crossed his face. Then Gaffer said, 'We're only going to be here for a short while, so fuck off!'

Needless to say, the manager fucked off. People tend to when Gaffer tells them how it is.

Normally in a man's company I wouldn't let people speak like that, but Gaffer is different. Gaffer is Gaffer. And the more I got to know him, the more I understood that the manager's approach was making him feel embarrassed and uncomfortable so he wanted out of that situation as fast as possible.

Gaffer's been in prison a lot. He did fourteen years last time and swears he was set up by some 'Northern shit' and that's made him bitter – especially about Northerners. He says he helped and trusted someone he shouldn't have. Now he says, 'I never trust a Northerner.' He believes that

Londoners who go to the North should respect their way of doing things – and very much vice versa.

'I said to these guys from Manchester, Kate, I said, "If I went to Manchester from London could I be the guv'nor?" They said, "No fucking way." So I said, "Well, it's the same here. If you're in London from the North, you should respect what Londoners are."'

Gaffer can talk the hind leg off a donkey and has an opinion on just about everything. He's done the lot. He's even been in politics. Believe it or not, he was a councillor and he got to meet Margaret Thatcher. God only knows what Maggie made of him. He is a wise-cracking gangster, if there is such an animal. But don't let his cheap gags fool you – he can be very menacing.

He's very alert when you meet him. He can sense trouble in the air before any other man. He says that when he's out, he likes to make sure he sits in a corner, he keeps his head down and he avoids unnecessary eye contact.

I visited his home and he has decorated his kitchen with crushed Coke cans and Kellogg's cornflake packets. In his garden there are 'gravestones' engraved with the names of people he'd like to see gone ... I think there's a lot of anger in Gaffer and he is ever so slightly off his fucking rocker.

'PS, Gaffer. Why are you called Gaffer?'

'My ex-father-in-law bought a business for me to run, a hairdresser's called Gaffer's. The name stuck.'

Oh.

BACKGROUND

I was born in Chelsea. My mother was Irish, my father was French. I was put in a home from the age of six months, a place called Tudor Lodge in Putney. And that's why I hate the Irish and the French because when I was born, she fucked off back to Ireland and he fucked off back to France. I haven't got brothers and sisters as such, but because I lived with families like the Richardsons their family became my family.

I was in the home until I was seven, then I was fostered out to a family called Rollinson. I was always fighting as a kid. The reason the Rollinsons fostered me was because they had a son who was being bullied at school and my foster mum, Florence, wanted someone to look after him. My foster father was at the home and he saw me having a fight with five people because they were bullying someone and he said, 'I'll have him. If he can fight like that, he can look after my son.'

LIFE OF CRIME

I've been to prison lots of times, I can't count how many times. I've only been in prison for violence, although my last one was for possession of drugs. I was disgusted with myself and that is the thing that turned my life around because I'm not a drug-dealer.

IS PRISON A DETERRENT?

No – it's a college. You get a petty crime-type person and he goes inside and he learns better things. So prison to me is a college. I've got a fucking degree!

DO YOU BELIEVE IN CAPITAL PUNISHMENT?

Yes – for paedophiles and for murder, by which I mean cases when people go around to other people's houses with the intent to murder. Not accidental murder. That don't count. Well, of course it does, but sometimes accidents happen.

The majority of crime doesn't deserve the death penalty, but child abuse is different. For that, yes, capital punishment. Get rid of the vermin – why keep them banged up? It's just going to cost the tax-payer more money. Kill the scum in the worst, the most painful way possible. Make them suffer the way they made the poor child suffer.

WHAT WOULD HAVE DETERRED YOU FROM A LIFE OF CRIME?

I never thought I was living a life of crime. I was born fighting and being nicked is part and parcel.

HAVE YOU EVER BEEN STABBED/SHOT?

I've been stabbed four times and I've had a shot taken at me. Another time, someone went to shoot me and the gun jammed. When that fella was going to shoot me, for one second I did shit myself but when the gun didn't go off, I looked at him and I said, 'Try again and see if it goes off.' But he didn't. So I winked at him and said, 'My turn.'

(Shortly before this book first went to print, a professional hit was put out on Gaffer. Two men on motorbikes pulled up alongside him and tried to shoot him – they failed.)

SCARIEST MOMENT?

Being sent back to the children's home.

SADDEST MOMENT?

I've had a lot of sad moments, so I won't say the saddest. I've had too many sad moments. I'll tell you that when I give someone my loyalty, I give them my loyalty, and there's only one person who can break that and that's them. And when they do, that's a sad moment because they've now got an enemy.

WHAT RATTLES YOUR CAGE?

Disrespectful people, people who see you've got something and they want it but it's yours and they should respect that and leave well alone.

HAVE YOU EVER REALLY LOVED ANYONE?

My ex-wife Wendy and my current girlfriend, Donna. I love her deeply, deeply.

157

WHAT FRIGHTENS YOU?

Losing Donna... Apart from that, nothing. I get frightened sometimes when my girlfriend's out and I'm not with her. If anything happened to her, I know I would kill the man and then I'd go away. I know I'd kill them. That frightens me sometimes.

DESCRIBE A HARD BASTARD

I don't think I'm a hard bastard. But to me a hard bastard is a man who knows he's got the strength but he only uses force, violence, as a last resort, when he has to. In my mind, nobody is a hard bastard, they've always got a weak point.

People often say, 'Oh, so-and-so, he's a hard bastard,' but my first reaction is to say, 'How do you know? Do you know this for yourself first-hand?'

I remember when I was at the Ministry of Sound once and I pulled this geezer because of what he'd done to a friend of mine. Everyone said he was a hard bastard but he wasn't. I've got a megaphone in my car and I got the megaphone and shouted through it so everyone could hear, 'You're nothing but a worthless piece of shit! Come out, you wanker!' He was standing there by his car and did nothing.

I don't think of being a hard bastard, but when a job has got to be finished, it's got to be finished.

Let me explain. This man was shot three times and I met the man who shot him and he said to me, 'It was just a warning.'

No, he was wrong. I said to him, 'In my eyes, one up into the air and a gun to the head is a warning – right? But you shoot a man three times and he's still alive in a year's time? That has now become an old score which has to be settled.'

In my eyes, if you shoot someone, you've got to shoot to kill because, if you don't, that person will be looking in the mirror every day, looking at their scar and they'll be thinking, This isn't right. They'll want revenge and, if you've done the shooting, there will be a time when you are vulnerable. There will be a time when you're off guard. But that person will be on guard, he's still got you in mind, he'll always have you in mind. You'll always have to watch your back, all day, all night, every day, every night.

NAME A HARD BASTARD

Dennis Richardson – known as one-hit Dennis.

HOW DO YOU SEE YOURSELF IN FIVE YEARS?

The one thing I've always maintained is that I won't die of natural causes.

ANY REGRETS?

No, I don't think so. The way I see it is: what will be will be. I have a lot of regrets but I can't change what's happened.

Charlie
Seiga

Charlie Seiga's reputation is awesome, both in Liverpool where he comes from and around London. He was once one of the most dangerous men in Britain. Many men were murdered on Charlie's patch and many times the police marked him out as a killer. They even codenamed him Killer and, later, Charlie called his autobiography just that. The killings, I'd heard, were swift, brutal and brilliantly organised.

The victims had all been liberty-takers, vicious bullies, scumbags and no-marks. Charlie has been called a contract killer, a hit-man, a murderer. He's also been accused of being the brains behind bank raids, armed robberies and wage snatches which netted hundreds of thousands of pounds.

He's a straight-talking man with a code of conduct he lives his life by and, more importantly, he expects everyone else to live by it, too. He has no time for people who pick on the defenceless, the weak, the vulnerable, the elderly or women. In that, he's a villain of the old school.

I arranged to meet Charlie on a Thursday afternoon at my publisher's office in London. When I got there, Charlie was waiting for me, leaning back nonchalantly on a swivel chair. Being a gentleman, he got up as soon as I walked in and greeted me by kissing my hand.

From that moment on, I didn't say much. Charlie talked, I listened. I watched him in that swivel chair, swinging non-stop from side to side, as he chatted and chatted in his Scouse accent, in a dialect that's completely alien to me.

When Charlie took a breath I tried to interrupt, but it was no use. Charlie was on a roll. He took a copy of my book, *Hard Bastards*, and started to give his opinion of the men in it. This one was a 'juiced-up doorman'; another was a 'waster'; that one was 'a soft lad'.

'They'd all be eaten alive in the 'Pool,' he said.

I started to get aggravated and twiddled my pen. I interrupted again – but I chose my moment carefully. 'Do you want to be in my book or not?'

He ummed and aahed. I could see him thinking, Shall I? Shan't I? He wasn't sure.

Five minutes, ten minutes. He chatted on. He told me about himself and there was no doubt that he was one hard man – he deserved to be in my book. But still he wasn't sure. Finally I said, 'Well, are you going to be my Northern hard man or not?'

He smiled. Yes.

Later, I learnt why he held back. Charlie doesn't want to be portrayed as a hard man because he says he's not a tough guy. I gave my word that I wouldn't distort the way I saw him and I won't... But...

He is a man who has done a lot of things in his life, always for a good reason – in his eyes. The way I see it, he's no angel. Then again, he's no devil either. We'll leave it at that. One thing for sure is that he is a gentleman. Recently, I had to go to Liverpool and Charlie and his friends met me. There was a limo waiting at the station and I have to say that I was treated like a princess.

Maybe it's called Liverpudlian hospitality. I'm not sure... Devil? Killer? But a gentleman, definitely.

BACKGROUND

I was born in Huyton, Liverpool, and I wasn't born into a life of crime – far from it. Both my parents were as straight as they come. They were both honest, hard-working people. My mother ran a fish and chip shop.

We were a big family, I had six brothers and one sister, but my mother made sure we were always well dressed, unlike a lot of the other poor kids. Growing up as a child in Huyton in the forties and early fifties was great for me and my brothers. We were all comfortable and happy at home and we young ones wanted for nothing.

I became a villain from the age of twelve. I think from an early age I wanted the good things in life, like fine clothes, cars and holidays. I had no intention whatsoever of earning my living honestly. I left school with no qualifications but I was still offered the opportunity of learning a trade such as plumbing, bricklaying or joinery. But that wasn't the life for me.

LIFE OF CRIME

If I were to list everything I have ever done or been involved in or charged with, believe me, the list would be endless. I am no angel and I was obviously involved in a wide range of criminal activities for a long time. I have been charged with using and being in possession of firearms and other weapons such as hatchets, machetes and knives. I've been charged for GBH several times, as well as threats to kill, attempted murder and murder. I've been questioned many, many times. But the only convictions I have are three GBHs, the last of them being in 1966 – that's more than thirty-five years ago.

DO YOU THINK PRISON IS A DETERRENT?

It is and it isn't – it all depends on you. It's a matter of opinion, that. Personally, I don't think so – you learn more about crime inside than out.

DO YOU BELIEVE IN CAPITAL PUNISHMENT?

Yes, I do for child molesting – not even killing a child, just touching a child – I'd kill them myself. Anybody who hurts children, in my eyes, just wants putting down. In fact, if I were in control of this country I might not even kill them – I'd just use them like animals are used for medical experiments. Instead of using the poor little animals, use those perverts, the real thing.

WHAT WOULD HAVE DETERRED YOU FROM A LIFE OF CRIME?

Perhaps if I'd been born rich, things might have been different... I don't know. Things have changed so much. There's no respect left. There's no law and order. If you get into a row with someone over a little scratch on a car bumper, you're in real trouble.

But a woman gets raped around the corner or an old man gets mugged and the guilty get nothing, no punishment. Morals have gone. When I was a young man and I was a robber, I chose that path. My parents were good, clean-living, honest people, but I didn't want to be clocking on at the factory and paying the mortgage for the rest of me life. I wanted more than that. There's no excuse for that.

In my day, you could walk in and out of a job. There was plenty of work for everyone. I chose my life, nobody corrupted me – it was all down to me.

HAVE YOU EVER BEEN STABBED/SHOT?

Yes, I've been stabbed, shot, mutilated, tortured, my lips torn off.

SCARIEST MOMENT?

Recently, I was tricked into going into this house in Liverpool. I got through the door of this house and I was attacked by a gang of drug-crazed scum, all off their heads on smack, crack and whatever else.

That was one of the scariest moments of my life because, let's face it, we're all scared of dying at times. We've all got to die sometime; it's just a question of when and where.

So I was ambushed by these guttersnipes – they're not interested in what or who you are – they're guttersnipes. They'll come out and pick on anyone – women, children, they don't care. I was sitting in the chair, having been wrapped up and scalded and the skin was dropping off me. I was there for hours.

The next day, they realised who I was and this big fella comes over and says, 'Listen, we respect you, Charlie man. But you're going to come back with us and we're goin' to whack you, we're goin' to do you.'

He pulled out a gun. And I'm tied up in this chair, ribs broken, stabbed, I'm done in, everything. I said, 'Listen...' I was still trying to be a man, but I was shitting myself ... I was scared ... and I said, 'Don't do this. I've got a little daughter, she's got a right to a father ... don't do this ... don't do me in the face ... she'll have to identify the body ... shoot me in the heart.'

Then, just as he was about to pull the trigger, the little scum who tricked me in the first place jumped up and said, 'Don't kill him here, for fuck's sake, don't kill him here. His daughter has seen him getting in the car outside the house.'

So I had a stay of execution. I was scared, but then they were full of apologies, like they are when they've got off the drugs.

I'll never forget that.

SADDEST MOMENT?

That was when my sister died. At the time, I was charged with attempted murder and I was on the run. All the police in the North-West were looking for me, even the ports were blocked off down South. It was serious.

I'd stopped this man; he was an animal, a woman-beater. I was going to give myself up. I knew I was going to prison, but my sister was dying of cancer. She was an angel, she was, never did anyone any harm in her life.

So I went to see her in hospital where she was dying of cancer and I knew I was giving myself up in an hour's time. And she's sitting up in the ward and all her friends were saying, 'Where's Charlie?'

Then I walked in with the flowers and she said, 'Oh God, Charlie!'

And I looked at her and I knew I wasn't going to see her again. When I turned away to leave, she said, 'Charlie!' but I didn't turn around because the tears were welling up and I didn't want her to see me. I didn't want her to see me crying. I was trying to be a man.

WHAT RATTLES YOUR CAGE?

Lots of things. Liars. I hate liars. And what rattles my cage more than anything is a lack of manners. We've all been brought up by good, decent people and we are decent people in our own way. OK, so I might have been a villain, a gangster, whatever you like to call it – I'm not now – but people seem to take that as leave to be rude.

I hate people who underestimate your manners, your cleanness, all those things.

HAVE YOU EVER REALLY LOVED ANYONE?

Yes. On many occasions. I love women. My first great love was when I was seventeen. I met this smashing girl in the heart of Liverpool. But I was wanted by the police so we had to get out. We decided to go on holiday – but who goes on holiday in the winter? We didn't know where to go.

I was going around with £1,000 in my pocket and it's 1958. A lot of money. So we went over to the Isle of Man.

We loved one another, we'd plan the future and things like that. I'd known girls before but this was the real thing, it was magic. She died tragically soon afterwards and I was shattered.

WHAT FRIGHTENS YOU?

I wouldn't like to end up like John Gotti in a cage. I wouldn't want to go back to prison. I wouldn't want to go back for one day, one hour. That's my biggest fear.

But I know that if I lost it, I could kill somebody – and I would if somebody touched my daughters or my family or my close friends. I'd go out and kill them and I'd think, Fuck the law, fuck the consequences. That's what I'm scared of.

DESCRIBE A HARD BASTARD

A hard bastard can be five foot three, he doesn't have to be six foot six. I know a man in Liverpool now who's five foot four and he's got the strength of ten men. He's a lovely, lovely man, lovely manners, but he's striped people, stabbed people and, to me, he is the hardest bastard I've ever met. People always underestimate him; he's a businessman. I wouldn't call myself a hard bastard. I'm not such a hard-case.

NAME A HARD BASTARD

There're so many, it's impossible to name just one. These are men who don't go round looking to make a reputation; they don't boast, they don't have to.

WHERE DO YOU SEE YOURSELF IN FIVE YEARS?

On a yacht in the Med – surrounded by beautiful women!

ANY REGRETS?

No, it's my life, I wouldn't swap it for the world. I've sampled everything, I've been to the best countries, had the best jewellery, best cars. I've got three lovely daughters – one's a lawyer, one's a jeweller and one's in the medical profession. No regrets – I've had a fantastic time.

I've written my own epilogue and this is it:

Throughout my criminal career, I was very loyal to my own kind or, should I say, anyone who was involved with me in any criminal activity. I always made sure when planning and executing any sort of robbery, or any other crime, my friends and family who were involved with me could rest assured that their liberty would never be jeopardised. If the work we were carrying out did not look right, even if a blade of grass was out of place, I would insist we pull out. After all, my top priority was to stay free and thieve another day.

I am fully aware that certain people have branded me a 'killer'. I would like to state I am not a psychopath. I would not get a thrill out of killing someone just for the sake of it. I am not a callous or cold-blooded person. I love my family and true friends to whom I would give my undying loyalty. I believe nearly every one of us, especially men, has the killer instinct in us. How many people can honestly say they have never thought about having, or would like to have, somebody killed? To kill someone is easy. The hardest part is the planning and organisation and getting away with it.

My only regret is there are four or five people

who are scum-dog enemies of mine and still living who shouldn't be, in my eyes. I would have no compassion or hesitation to have them killed but, like I say, it's the getting away with it afterwards.

Revenge is sweet. As long as I get revenge, no matter how long it takes, to me it is the most satisfying sensation there is. Certain people have given me secondary information, of course, that I am going to be shot or killed. All I can say to that, to whoever they are, is – make sure you plan it properly and make sure you've got the bottle to put one in my head instead of half-heartedly in my leg. If you are going to do the job, do it properly. After all, we have all got to die sometime. It's just a matter of when and where. Maybe one day my luck will run out. Well, if that is the case, so be it.

Ian Wadley

Ian Wadley is a big, powerful black man. You'd never knock this man over – he's solid all over, as wide as he's tall. When he was doing five years for armed robbery, he met a screw called Gary Taylor who recognised his natural strength and encouraged him in body-building and weight-lifting. Since then he's been in championship contests for both – he's lifted six hundred kilos! – and it shows. Ian is fit, although not as fit as he was. In November 2000, he was shot in the back and leg when someone tried to murder him. He's also been axed in the leg and stabbed three times.

When I first met him, I didn't think he looked like an Ian. His looks and size and power just don't suit the name. I thought he should be called something else – Razor, for example! He didn't agree with me.

Instead, I nicknamed him Prada because of the way he looks, the smart way he dresses; his image is so important to him. He's got to have the best of everything. He's got over forty thousand pounds' worth of clothes in his wardrobe, all the best designer gear – suits, shoes, the lot. I can't imagine Ian would ever wear anything from Marks & Spencer! When he goes out, he really does look the biz! So, I call him Prada.

Ian is a hard bastard, no doubt about it – he's been picked up for three murders, not to mention the armed robberies. But behind the toughness there's real gentleness. He's so quiet and polite, almost humble. In my experience, they are the most dangerous.

And he's obviously madly in love with his girlfriend Sarah, a gorgeous Page 3 girl and lap-dancer – he can't watch her when she dances at the club. He waits upstairs while she's doing her turn. (I watched and she was amazing – like Olga Korbut on acid!)

Ian couldn't have been more helpful when he appeared in my first TV series of *Hard Bastards*. He let me into all parts of his life. He let me see his world, his house, his business, his gym and he's an extraordinary man, the kind who sets himself a goal and goes all out to achieve it. Then, having done that, he drops it and goes on to the next goal. Always higher, always better, always more.

He let me into his world, but I couldn't help feeling that Ian is a very secretive man; he plays his cards close to his chest. I know he is a dangerous man but I didn't see him as intimidating. And yet … and yet … I felt there were deep, dark secrets that I hadn't yet uncovered. Secrets that I couldn't – or Ian wouldn't let me – uncover.

BACKGROUND

I've got brothers and sisters but I was lonely as a boy. I don't want to say why I was unhappy, I just was. It upsets me to think about it, let alone talk about it.

LIFE OF CRIME

I've been in prison for an armed robbery. My job was to go in there and get the safe out – that was my main job. I got five years for that. I've been arrested three times for murder, once for armed robbery. Shootings, stabbings, things like that, mainly being in the wrong place at the wrong time. Honest!

IS PRISON A DETERRENT?

No. But I wouldn't want to go back inside. Having said that, I'm old-fashioned. If it was a friend, or someone I'd known for a long time, and they were in trouble, I would go out of my way to do something to help them, whatever that meant. I would probably regret my actions because it would be a long time inside or whatever ... I'd stop and think ... but I'd probably stop and think after the crime.

DO YOU BELIEVE IN CAPITAL PUNISHMENT?

No. Well, yes and no. It depends on the crime. My answer would probably be yes if it was a child molester or something like that, or someone who was going around raping kids. If it were a daughter of mine, I'd kill him myself. But anything else ... it's a difficult question, isn't it? Getting rid of someone full-stop.

WHAT WOULD HAVE DETERRED YOU FROM A LIFE OF CRIME?

A better upbringing, I suppose. It's the way I was brought up. I come from a working background. My dad was a builder and plumber – now, in some families they'll push their sons and daughters in the right direction, but in our family, my dad was all 'Do this' and 'Do that' and a few years ago my old man said, 'No one's taking my place' or whatever and my brother said, 'Well, push us in the right direction.' He could have done, but it wasn't like that in our family. And that's why I took to crime and things like that.

But I suppose I'm too old to make excuses now. It's not just about money – if I'd been pushed in the right direction, I would have got a better education, a better job. As it was, I ended up doing silly jobs like being a 'gofer' – all sorts. I worked for Barclays Bank for a few weeks, as it happens!

HAVE YOU EVER BEEN STABBED/SHOT?

I've been stabbed in the arm, stabbed in the tops of my legs, I've been shot in the legs and I've still got a bullet in the kneecap. I've been shot in the back and macheted in the leg. Yes, I've been through it all.

SCARIEST MOMENT?

I should say being shot is my scariest moment. Being shot is pretty scary.

SADDEST MOMENT?

I'd rather not say.

WHAT RATTLES YOUR CAGE?

Not much. Except bullies. Bullies rattle my cage. They have ever since I was bullied as a boy.

HAVE YOU EVER REALLY LOVED ANYONE?

Sarah, my girlfriend, my partner. I've been straight with her, I've told her everything. She knows everything about me. I know everything about her. We have a really good relationship because it's based on trust.

WHAT FRIGHTENS YOU?

Sarah and rats! I do like to go out with my mates but people will always rat on me to Sarah! Nine times out of ten, if I go to a club there's a friend of Sarah's working there! Perhaps I spend too long speaking to one girl – and they rat on me! That's frightening!

DESCRIBE A HARD BASTARD

Most hard bastards are quiet but there's something about them; it's the way they walk, their presence, their aura, people around you know if you've got it, they can feel it.

NAME A HARD BASTARD

Johnny Adair. I know some Irish people who know him and if you do something to him, he'll come back to you the next day. He's a fearsome, fearless man. Do something to him and he'll come after you and I do respect him.

WHERE DO YOU SEE YOURSELF IN FIVE YEARS?

Owning a couple of villas, hopefully settling down, getting married. Having a good family life, really – that's the most important thing.

ANY REGRETS?

No regrets at all. No. Being in prison taught me how to survive on the street. If I never achieve anything then I'll have regrets, but so far I have none. I've achieved things. I've travelled all over the world. I've done my fair share of things on my own so I haven't got any regrets.

I wouldn't mind going into films but nothing major – a small part or something would be good – I'd like to be an actor, but nothing major – an *EastEnders* role maybe! Or perhaps I could work for Guy Ritchie or someone like that!

Gary Hunter

Meeting Gary Hunter – ex-soldier and now minder to the rich and famous – was an odd experience.

I sipped my caffe latte in the lounge of a posh hotel waiting for Gary to arrive. I glanced at my watch. Bang on 7.00 p.m. – the appointed time – the automatic doors opened and there he stood. Not what I expected, not at all. He was small and wiry with penetrating blue eyes.

From the moment he sat down, he didn't stop talking. Usually, I'm the one who does most of the talking! But not this time. Gary wasn't the run-of-the-mill hard man I'm used to interviewing. He was different. Of course we've all got our own opinions about politics and the like, but his ideas consumed him; he was anti-Government, anti-establishment, anti-just-about-everything.

He was very well versed in Army matters. He knew all about 'covert operations', 'intelligence surveillance', gadgets and guns. He spoke at length about things I'd never given any thought to and he gave me answers to questions I'd never even asked. Yes, he was different; thought-provoking, intensely passionate about his beliefs, banging the table with his fists to emphasise a point – spilling my caffe latte in the process then mopping it up without drawing breath.

As we left the hotel, I asked him where his car was parked. He pointed to a dimly lit side road beyond the hotel forecourt.

'I was here an hour before you,' he whispered. 'I sussed the joint out and watched you arrive.'

He shook his head at me and smiled a strange smile: 'Well,' he said, 'better the hunter than the hunted ...'

BACKGROUND

I was brought up in a little fishing village on the east side of Scotland, but I suppose my accent has changed because no one down here in the South knows I'm a Scot. Even so, my accent comes right back when I talk to my father!

The village was divided into four areas with invisible boundaries, and groups from each used to fight each other. I ended up fighting the lot!

I was an only child and I trained in the martial arts from the age of nine. I did Thai boxing for eight years. I've fought in France, Belgium, Denmark and Holland.

I got married last year and I've got one child, a beautiful little girl.

LIFE OF CRIME
Nothing much I've ever been caught for. I've been arrested on several occasions for violence. My prison record reads nothing else – violence.

IS PRISON A DETERRENT?
No. I've only done time on remand, so obviously I can't speak for long-term prisoners. But, from what I've seen inside, all they try to do is destroy your train of thought. They do your thinking for you. They give you breakfast at half-eight, dinner at twelve, tea at five – it's up to you to keep your mind working while you're inside.

Prison didn't deter me from anything – it's other people in the business who have deterred me. I think in this day and age there're so few people you can trust – people you can trust just aren't out there anymore. I've seen some people fuck over their best mate for a pound note and that's not the way I was brought up, that never happened then. Money has become more important than friendship. People's loyalties seem to be determined by one thing only – and that's money.

DO YOU BELIEVE IN CAPITAL PUNISHMENT?
Yes. I was brought up with the belt. I believe in an eye for an eye and a tooth for a tooth. I don't believe in hanging for murder – I think they should be put through what their victims were put through.

It's crazy. Someone bursts into your house so you bash them up – but you're not supposed to do that no more, are you? You're supposed to pick up the phone and say, 'Look, there's someone in my house. Can you come round here and get them out?'

Well, that isn't a natural human instinct if someone is threatening your family and children. It's like with an animal – if you try and take its young, it will go for you. We think we're so much better as human beings, but we're not.

I don't believe capital punishment should be by lethal injection – that's just putting them to sleep. That's what we do to pets in pain – pets that we love. Why should you give that to someone who's done something really bad? I believe in the very, very old ways.

WHAT WOULD HAVE DETERRED YOU FROM A LIFE OF CRIME?

I don't think I've had a life of crime. We've all done things illegally, obviously. What is crime? It's what the Government tells you is crime. They say you can't do that, so it's a crime. Just because they say it isn't right to do it, doesn't mean that, in my eyes, it's not right to do it. What they say is a crime I don't necessarily see as a crime. I earn my living my way because they won't let me earn it any other way.

HAVE YOU EVER BEEN STABBED/SHOT?

I've been stabbed and I've been shot. I have a hole in the bottom of my back and in my nipple and at the back of my head.

SCARIEST MOMENT?

It was in a club in Colchester and a big group of doormen had come up there for a stag night. This one big geezer was threatening a little geezer – he was bullying him and there's no need to bully anyone, there's no reason to invade anyone else's space. So I said, 'Come on, mate, leave it. He's only half your size so there's no need to pick on him. Go and pick on someone your own size.'

He was a fucking big bastard and he said he couldn't give a shit.

He walked off but then I saw him in the corner with six others, all big lads, and I was on my own. So I went behind the bar. Suddenly they came rushing at me behind the bar, they knocked the doorman out and I was alone with eleven of them. I escaped to the kitchen but they followed me. I got in a few punches but they were hitting me with everything – fire extinguishers, soup ladles, you name it. That's where I got all the cuts on the back of my head, but I never actually went down.

Then one of them tried to rob my pockets and that did it.

I managed to kick one and punch another and that gave me a bit of space so I could run off down the corridors, slamming all the doors behind me. I had blood coming out everywhere.

Then I got into the toilets and there was a skylight with wired glass in it – and that was the only way out. There was a bang on the door. I opened the door and hit him. He went down. His mate was outside in the corridor running up and down – it was only a matter of time.

I managed to punch my way through the skylight. I cut my hand to fuck, but at least I got out on the roof. From there I could see them come out the back and one of them said, 'Oh fuck it, the little bastard's scared, he's fucked off.'

Well, that was enough for me. I jumped off the roof into the lot of them. I nutted one, hit another, then jumped over the fence into a garden and off. They followed and there were two of them faster than the others – it's always the way, Kate. There're always two who are faster than the rest. So I stopped and hit both of them.

I got away. But, I tell you, when I was actually trapped in that kitchen, I was scared. That was one of the scariest moments of my life because I was getting it from all angles.

SADDEST MOMENT?
My mum died of cancer when I was twenty-one.

WHAT RATTLES YOUR CAGE?
Bullies. You see these so-called hard men and they're not hard men, they're bullies. There's no such thing as a hard man. Every man's got a chin. All you've got to do is find his before he finds yours. It's up to you to prepare yourself to do that. There's no such thing as a lucky

punch – well, maybe sometimes but very rarely. It's up to you to know what you're capable of and to do it. But if you go into a fight thinking you're better than the next man you'll lose anyway.

HAVE YOU EVER REALLY LOVED ANYONE?

Yes, big-time. I love my wife, Jo. Our relationship was on and off for a few years but I'm married to her now.

I suppose the person I have loved most was me mum, maybe because I didn't have brothers and sisters. I was really close to her. I was outraged when she died of breast cancer. She never smoked, never drank, never did a bad thing in her life. She had both breasts removed, then all her hair went. I felt helpless, outraged to witness what that did to her as a woman. I was a nasty person then. I was the nastiest person I knew then, I was the kind of person I'd hate now. I couldn't understand why it was happening, I didn't give a fuck about anything or anyone.

DESCRIBE A HARD BASTARD

I'm ex-military and I'd describe a hard bastard as someone who can cope with all sorts – extremes of temperature, hot and cold, near-starvation, being able to go on when you can't go on no more. When it comes to a fight, how many fights last longer than a few minutes? Very few. I admire boxers. You look at a professional boxer, how long is he fighting for? He's got to dig deep like he's never dug before. Each round is three minutes. People think that's nothing, but it's a lot. You get the average man off the street and tell him to punch a bag, shadow box, for three minutes and he won't be able to do it.

A hard man to me is definitely a man who doesn't use a tool. Don't get me wrong, there're times when you have got to use tools, but a hard man, if there's a row, he'll fight you toe to toe – he won't pull out a knife and kill you. A hard man can stand there and he'll take a punch but he'll get over that and he'll return it back.

NAME A HARD BASTARD

Rocky Marciano.

WHERE DO YOU SEE YOURSELF IN FIVE YEARS?

If only we knew where we'd be in five years! Well, there's only one person it depends on – it's up to me. There're so many people wandering around with no direction. It's up to you to make your future. I've got a direction.

When I first came out of the services, I found civilian life fucking boring; there was nothing to do. I was in for six years and what I've done is turn around all that knowledge and use it. I still keep up the fitness; I train all the time. Of course, in the services, you're told what to do, you get your orders for the day, but you don't mind doing it because you know that the people who are telling you have been through it themselves.

I know what I did in the Marines and I know I'm good at what I do. I've used that. Now I do bodyguarding, I'm working to get my certificate with the SAS up in Hereford because it's the only one that's recognised within the industry. It's not like the normal nine-to-five job and yes, there's aggression involved, but that's all I've ever done. I went straight from school into the forces, then I did my Marine course, then I became a PT instructor and then my mum developed cancer and that's why I left. If that hadn't happened, I'd still be in the Marines because I loved it. I travelled the world, I've been all over the world – Far East, everywhere.

I've always had a sense of adventure. Maybe it's to do with being an only child. If you've got brothers and sisters, you've always got someone to play with; if you're an only child, you've got to find someone to go and play with, which I think makes you an outgoing person anyway. I have a direction and I'm happy with that direction.

ANY REGRETS?

Yes, I regret giving my friendship to some people who I now know didn't deserve it. I gave my loyalty, I'd have given my life for these people and I thought they would have done the same for me.

I can't say if I've done things I regret, I suppose the answer to that must be yes and no. I rarely do things I regret because I think things through carefully before I do them. That's training, I suppose. I don't really act on impulse and I don't have time for regrets. It's all down to yourself.

For example, you can't get grassed up. If you get grassed up, it means that you've told them or you've told someone who's told them. It's up to you. The only person responsible for your life is yourself. If you give your word to a best mate, then you've got to think, 'Can I trust them?' There's not that many people out there you can give your word to.

If you only give that word to yourself, then you've only got yourself to worry about and if you work alone, you won't get caught because nobody knows – the only person who can get you caught is you – nobody else can. People say, 'You grassed me up' – I'll say, 'You grassed yourself up, you stupid mug.'

It's like a chain. The shorter and fatter a chain, the stronger it is – the longer it is, the thinner it is, the weaker it is. That's why you keep things to yourself. The more you tell other people, the weaker that chain is. And that's how I've always lived. And that's why I haven't done any bird.

Sid the
Knife

**Sid the Knife... just the name conjures up all kinds of
things you'd rather not think about.**

We went to meet him at a service station on the M25
on a horrible, rainy Tuesday night and were just having
a cup of coffee when in walked two policemen, then
another two, and they sat at a table behind us.

This wouldn't do. There was no way that Sid would
talk with four Old Bill sitting immediately behind him;
he'd feel decidedly uncomfortable. Then in came another
two and joined the others and now there were six.

I moved tables – and just in time, for in walked Sid – a
six-foot-something black man with long dreadlocks and,
I have to admit, a shifty look on his face.

He said quietly he'd left his tools in the car – he felt
naked without them. It was the first time he'd gone in
anywhere without a tool for years. I was slightly uneasy
– all I knew about him was his name.

But he turned out to be not what I expected at all. He was so polite, so respectful, a pleasure to talk to. What impressed me was that he seemed so aware of how people could look at him and get the wrong idea – i.e. feel a bit scared. He said that when he walked down the road, he always crossed to the other side if there was a woman walking ahead – he didn't want to alarm her.

He honestly respects women and he talked a lot about his mother. He said it was a privilege to talk to me – which was nice – and he talked about the respect he had for Ron, because he had set standards for the underworld which were based on respect. Sid is a very moral man, a deep thinker – and, as he liked to put it, without morals 'it's a dog-eat-dog world'.

He didn't like criticising people without knowing them – he likes to make up his own mind about people. He doesn't like gossip or hearsay. If someone says someone is a wrong 'un, he'll decide for himself whether it's true. He won't be told – make a friend of Sid and you've got a friend for life.

He had a lovely sense of humour. He said, 'I suppose you want to photograph me with a big knife!'

'Yes, please.' I grinned.

In fact, I was surprised he agreed to be in this book at all, but he laughed and said, 'You're nobody unless you're in somebody's book these days!'

Oh.

The more we talked, the more I puzzled about his

nickname – Sid the Knife. He just didn't look or sound like a mad knifeman to me.

'I used to like a bit of Charlie in the past,' he confessed. 'I used to snort it off a knife, a small knife, so I'd carry that knife with me. Then, as the lines got bigger, so did the knives! That's how it started, so I'm Sid the Knife...'

Well, that's a relief... I think!

BACKGROUND

I was born in south-east London then moved to the East End when I was about seven. I've got four brothers and two sisters. One brother and a sister are in the Caribbean, the others are here. My parents went back to the Caribbean for a while when I was growing up and I lived with a white foster family and their kids became my brothers as well. Because we were split up at times, I met my real brothers and sisters at different ages. I met one sister when I was eleven, met another brother when I was thirteen and another when I was fifteen.

I had a normal kind of upbringing; you know, going to school, doing sports, athletics and things. I always wanted to be a body-builder – even though I was six four, I wanted to be big! I remember seeing a geezer walking down the road when I was about fifteen and as he was getting closer to me, he was getting bigger and bigger. He had this little bag in his hand and I looked at him, at this huge geezer, and I thought, I want to look like that. So, from the age of fifteen, I started training.

As a child, I knew hardship; we didn't have holidays, no new shoes, that kind of thing, but it was a good life and I never begrudged my mum for not giving things to me because I could see, watching her struggle, that that's how life goes sometimes.

I used to have fights at school but I was respected as well. There weren't many black kids at school and I got problems in the third, fourth and fifth years. I suppose race and colour had something to do with it, but because I went to school with my white foster brothers we all dealt with it ourselves. I always tried to be friends with everyone. I was always friends with the girls!

At home, I've never believed in all that effing and blinding in front of your parents. If I had done that, my mum would have given me a clip round the ear! She'd still give me a clip round the earhole now! When you go in your mum and dad's house you've got to behave; when you walk in that door you've got to behave like a son. Whatever you do, you don't bring it home.

I left school young. My first job was working on a building site and I used to give my mum my wages every week. I always looked after my mum, that was my first priority. As a teenager, I was never one for going to football matches. From the age of fourteen, I was going to clubs locally and up the West End. I started working the door at seventeen.

One day, when I was training, I met Carlton Leach and we got talking. He said, 'Come on, I'll look after you, Son.' He taught me bits and pieces and I got introduced to loads of people. We're like family now – he's helped me through thick and thin. He's been there when things haven't worked out for me. He's met my mum and dad. They took him in and called him Son so, as far as I'm concerned, he's my brother. If my parents have given him that kind of recognition, that's good enough for me.

If there's anything I want to do – like this interview with you – I ask his permission. If there's anything I've got to do, like debt-collecting or personal minding or working the door, I talk to him first. Don't get me wrong, I've got my own views and he asks my opinion for certain things, too. But I feel it's a duty; if you're that close to someone, you can't simply go out doing your own thing ... respect. That's what it's all about. If you've not got that, then you have nothing.

LIFE OF CRIME

I've been arrested by the police but I've never been in court, never been nicked. I try to be as straight as possible because I've got no time to mess people about. I look at it this way: if you're in trouble and you need help, I won't turn my back on you, I'll help you out if I think it's right even if someone else says, 'Don't, they're no good.' If you ask me for help my loyalty goes right down to the end. People can say I'll die for you and all that, people can talk it and people can do it – I do it.

IS PRISON A DETERRENT?

It's a deterrent for the everyday, nine-to-five working person. It does deter those people. But, for people like us, it's like in the back of our minds. Whatever we do, we try and keep one step ahead of the Old Bill. That's the name of the game in our own community.

For a lot of people, prison is no deterrent at all, people like rapists and paedophiles. Prison doesn't deter them because they seem to be lost in their own world. I can't tolerate men who abuse women and children. I can't stand the fact that there are people out there doing things to these children. If a child molester lived round the corner, I'd knock at his house and I'd knock him out. Because, at the end of the day, that kid is my kid, even if I haven't got kids.

DO YOU BELIEVE IN CAPITAL PUNISHMENT?

Yeah. People say taking the law into your own hands is wrong, but what if it were a member of your own family? You'd want revenge. Then there are people like rapists, stalkers, people who hurt children. You have to have a line somewhere.

WHAT WOULD HAVE DETERRED YOU FROM A LIFE OF CRIME?

I've never had a life of crime as such. Crime has been around me and I've witnessed certain situations. But what is crime? It's easier to do something bad than to do something good. I mean, if there was a tenner on the floor, would you pick it up and hand it in? But how many people do that? It's easier to put it in your pocket. People say, 'I found it so it's mine,' but it ain't yours.

But to do something good like hand it in to the police station isn't easy and, if you do, people say you're mad! So what could have deterred me from doing that?

My life is what it is. It's got nothing to do with my family upbringing. Maybe if I'd had the opportunity to educate myself a lot more it would have been different, if I'd had the education to get a proper job, to establish myself on the ladder and go up in society. Maybe then I wouldn't be here now. I'd be out there earning loads of dough, living in a nice house, enjoying nice this, nice that and the other.

But these days, everyone seems to be going down the ladder towards crime. Everyone is thinking, I can earn a monkey tomorrow if I do that and who's going to know?

HAVE YOU EVER BEEN STABBED/SHOT?

Er … yes, come to think of it, I have been stabbed, many, many years ago. Does that count? I've been shot at as well.

SCARIEST MOMENT?

Scary moments are when you're trapped in a corner and you know there's only one way out. Or getting the phone call which says, 'You've got to go now.' That's the scariest moment. No matter how people say, 'Yeah, I'm up for it, I'm up for it,' it's scary.

You're sitting indoors, watching the telly and all of a sudden you get the phone call and someone says that whoever has been shot. Whatever you're doing, you think, Right, what have we got to do? All your emotions are suddenly tight. You might be feeling confident with ten people around you but this only involves you, you as an individual, and that's what's scary.

The scariest person is yourself because when you look in that mirror, there's only one person you see. When you open that door, who goes through that door? Only you go through that door, no one else. Whether you are asking for help, or going to give help, you are the only one who has to deal with problems at the end of the day.

SADDEST MOMENT?

Watching my cousin die of cancer. She was forty. I used to see my aunts and one day they turned up and said my cousin was ill. I went round to see her. My aunt said, 'When you go in and see her, be prepared.' I didn't understand what she meant, but when I went in the only thing I recognised was her voice. I hadn't seen her for about three months. Apparently, she'd been ill for a while and I knew she was losing weight. She went from about ten stone to about six stone.

She smiled and said, 'How're you doing?'

I said, 'Oh, all right,' but I felt like I'd seen a ghost. I felt all shaky inside like when you've got to go to court in the morning and you know you're going to get a ten-stretch or whatever. That shaky feeling before you get the cold sweats. Like after a big night out.

That was one of the worst experiences of my life because, just before she died, she came to me in a dream and asked me to let her go. I went to see her on the Monday, she came to me in the dream on the Tuesday and she died on the Thursday. It took me about a year to accept the fact that she had gone. I felt hopeless. Just hopeless.

WHAT RATTLES YOUR CAGE?

People who are going to do people wrong. Wrong 'uns. People who hurt children. People who scare people like women just walking down the road and they're scared of someone coming up behind them.

I remember, when I was sixteen, there was this old woman walking down the road and I had to cross the road to make her feel comfortable because I was a man walking down the road behind her. I knew what she was probably thinking. People who make old people think like that – they annoy me.

I always feel uncomfortable walking behind a woman, I feel I know what they're thinking and I have to make myself aware for them, I have to move that much away from them so they can feel comfortable. I feel it when they're walking towards me so I say excuse me or I walk in the road so they walk on without worrying. That could be my mother, my girlfriend, my daughter.

HAVE YOU EVER REALLY LOVED ANYONE?

Yeah, yeah, yeah, yeah. You can't beat love. Whatever people say about love these days, it's that emotional feeling that comes over you which you can't explain.

Men can't express their feelings, women can. But I've seen men kill themselves over women. I think love is the biggest emotion, it brings men to their knees. I've seen big men top themselves, I've seen big men overdose. I've had big men ring me up on the phone and say, 'I can't handle it no more, I'm going to shoot myself.'

Then I've had to go round his house and spend time with him. I'm in love now and I'm happier than I used to be because I've learnt to understand my stupid ways and learnt that my way of dealing with things hasn't always been right. So now I look at other angles and listen to what other people say and look at how I am when I'm in a relationship.

I can see what I used to do and I say to myself, 'Let's not do that now, let's have a good time. Let's have a laugh and a joke.' I've mellowed – I guess it comes with age!

WHAT FRIGHTENS YOU?

The fact of knowing that I've got to look over my shoulder when someone says, 'I'm going to come and get yer' – I can't stand that. I think if you're going to come and get someone, do it now because I've got no time to look over me shoulder. If that's the case, then I'll go and do it myself.

I suppose I'm a bit paranoid. Paranoia is paranoia and it does wind you up, but it helps; it helps because it keeps you aware of yourself all the time, keeps you asking questions.

DESCRIBE A HARD BASTARD

A hard person to me is someone who comes up to you and does what he does and then walks away and doesn't say anything about it. That's not using anything, whether it's his hands or fists or whatever. He just comes up to you and gives it to you and that's it. And that can be anyone; doesn't have to be the strongest man in the world, it can be the youngest kid.

NAME A HARD BASTARD

My mum. She is a born-again Christian now, but when I was younger, you didn't wanna mess with her. I would say my mum, then my dad.

WHERE DO YOU SEE YOURSELF IN FIVE YEARS?

Hopefully in the Caribbean, looking after my mum and dad, and settled with my girlfriend. I'll be looking back on my life and thinking I've had a good run.

ANY REGRETS?

No, not really. I wish I'd given a bit more back to my mum. I do regret not getting a better education. I'd like to have learnt to read and write a lot better. I should have educated myself a bit more – that's my regret. But I've got my education from people around me.

Baz Allen

Baz Allen is big and black and he constantly wears a black bowler hat. He reminds me of someone.

'Do you like *The Avengers*?' I ask.

'No, it's more of a James Bond thing,' he grins. 'It's more about me being available anywhere, any time, wherever, whatever. It's Baz for hire. It signifies that I'm a gentleman and a bowler is a British tradition.'

That's it! I've got it! Not Steed – Oddjob!

Baz is intelligent, charming, witty. He dresses like a City gent and he speaks like a City gent. From his reputation, I suppose I expected a bit of a thug, but he's not like that. He had real manners; he was sophisticated – Oddjob the Gentleman.

I'd noticed Baz at the endless gangsters' dos and book launches I'd been to. He cropped up everywhere. I didn't know anything about him, but then why should I? Then, while researching this book, I was looking through piles of photographs – gangsters, villains, hoodlums, tough guys of all shapes and sizes. There, time and time again, was this big black man in the bowler hat.

Who the hell was he? What does he do? Where does he come from? Who was this strange enigma in the bowler?

I started to make a few calls.

'Who's the big man in the smart suit?'

Answer: 'Don't know.'

'The one with a big smile?'

'Don't know.'

'The one with the bowler hat.'

'Oh ... you mean Baz Allen...'

There is no mistaking Baz and it made the job of finding him easy. Brilliant for me and for this book. But maybe not so good if I was a hitman or, even worse, God forbid, the Old Bill.

BACKGROUND

I've been around violence all my life. My father was violent. I watched my father beat my mother up. I used to watch him beat me up! The first time I remember being violent myself was when I was about six and there was this guy at school called Roy Jackson. He used to agitate me for some reason.

I was a bit over-sensitive and I remember the teacher separating me from him all the time. Then, one day, we were going home and I caught him on the fire escape. He grabbed me and I pushed him really hard down the stairs and he cracked the side of his head. I thought, Got you, you bastard!

That was the first time that I projected the violence I'd seen from my father on to someone else. It was a release for me. I was a frustrated little kid. When you're that young, you can't really explain how you feel, but you know you're frustrated. You're stressed out but you can't communicate – you can barely speak. I was like a little tornado!

I went on to the junior school, then the seniors, where I got suspended because I got into a fight with a teacher. He'd been picking on my sister – I've got two brothers and two sisters. I was suspended and the next day my parents took me to the school. I was told I had to apologise but I suppose I was being a bit arrogant about it because I refused. So they expelled me. And, of course, my dad gave me a hiding because I'd been expelled.

People say if you get bullied as a child you either supress your anger or it turns you the other way. I think my behaviour does stem from bullying when I was younger. I'm not making excuses – I'm just analysing it.

LIFE OF CRIME

I went to reform schools. The first thing I got nicked for was pinching milk bottles. All of us kids did it and then we'd go to a friend's house and have a fry-up! I think I got a caution for that.

Then I got pulled over after threatening someone with

a knife. I ended up before Highgate magistrates and got a year's conditional discharge. After that I went on to street robberies with my mates, street robberies with tear gas. I got sentenced to three and three concurrent for that. I kept the clipping out of the local newspaper and it read: TERROR FIRM GOES DOWN. Terror firm – we were only about seventeen!

Then we used to do wage snatches, shops, steaming – we probably started off the steaming in London. We'd be ten or fifteen guys who'd go steaming into stores and we'd have six or seven tills. Then there was burglary, doing a house – I got a 'short, sharp shock' for that. It started off as GBH, then went down to ABH. I came out of that and then did youth custody. Then, after that, no more time. I suppose I got wise. I put myself at the sharp end, but when I got involved I was very careful about everything I did.

IS PRISON A DETERRENT?

No.

I heard someone on the TV the other day saying we should give stiffer sentences: the three-strike rule, lock them up, make them work. But if you penalise someone, they rebel. They're not going to cave in and say, 'Oh, I'm never going to prison again.' People come out of prison vicious. They come out and they're nasty. They're more inclined not to leave bodies hanging about. If they go to a house or they go to a bank and it looks like a witness is there – he goes.

You've got to understand the person as well as the crime. You can't just throw huge sentences at them. You've got to show some kind of interest in them when they're in prison. Don't just bang them up or they'll turn to drugs. Education helps – you've got to get people actively involved in something. When you're banged up, it's bloody boring! Often people think that drugs is the only way they can get through their sentence. Then they still end up bullying or being bullied. They still end up raping or being raped. It just goes on. There's no change. Prison, as it is, is really no deterrent.

DO YOU BELIEVE IN CAPITAL PUNISHMENT?

Fucking hell! That's a bit coarse, isn't it? What happens if you never did it? What happens if you've been fitted up? It's an injustice and you're gone.

But child molesters... How do you deal with them? You can't keep locking them up then letting them out, then locking them up. They're filth, these people! I've got two sons, one of six and one of fourteen, and to be honest, if anything happened to them, people would go. You've got to electrocute these people. Just spark them up with a proper lorry battery, know what I mean?

WHAT WOULD HAVE DETERRED YOU FROM A LIFE OF CRIME?

I didn't get much attention shown to me when I was at school because, maybe, I was a bit of a disturbed child. But I was a bright lad, I loved poetry, literature, language.

I just didn't get the attention or encouragement. The teachers didn't have that way of dealing with people. I suppose if we'd had money it would have made a difference.

HAVE YOU EVER BEEN STABBED/SHOT?

I've been shot at. We were doing a recovery somewhere in Epping. Basically, we'd given the guy forty-eight hours to do something, to come up with the money and he hadn't. We got the sob story, took back what we could, there was fifteen grand in the house and we took that and we took his motor.

We were the other side of the A11, not going fast, when his friends appeared and suddenly the back window's gone out. They were obviously drugged up and they started trying to drive us off the road. So, yeah, I've been shot at and it's not as glamorous as you might see it on *Lock, Stock* and all that.

SCARIEST MOMENT?

It's difficult for me to explain without giving too much away, but I'll try... I think that was my scariest moment. We had to get someone back. They'd gone off with something. I turned up at the house where they were and this person was hell-bent on saying they didn't have what they had. They kept saying, 'I haven't got it, I haven't got it.'

They got a bit of a hiding and they were still saying they hadn't got it. It was getting to a point where a decision was going to be made and the people who were doing it weren't too solid on what they were doing, if you get my drift.

I wasn't sure whether they were going to end up doing something which would mean everyone getting life. That was a bit of a scary moment then.

SADDEST MOMENT?

My half-brother committed suicide. It was all because of a loving relationship. The girl he had been involved with didn't want him back – he was only in his teens. I've also got a top mate who's doing twenty and his mother was like a second mother to me. I watched her die slowly of cancer. She had breast cancer and they cut it out but it came back. Those are my saddest moments.

WHAT RATTLES YOUR CAGE?

Disrespect. I've been done for road rage, all kinds of shit and for what? For principles. I'm not rude, I'm polite but disrespect can rev you up.

Racial harassment doesn't really rattle my cage because, to be honest with you, I haven't received that much. Not since I was younger. But I remember when I was just thirteen being pulled by the Special Patrol Group. Me and my friend saw a car that had been dumped and it still had the speakers in so we took them. We knew a guy who'd buy them off us.

So we were walking along in our adidas jackets – we'd both walked into C&A, put them on and walked out again, which was the best way to do things in those days – and we were each carrying a speaker.

We bumped into the police. I threw my speaker over the fence but my friend Mike wanted to keep his. A police van pulled up and they put us in the van and I watched as one of the coppers put his gloves on. Suddenly, without warning, he grabbed me and he started to strangle me, I swear to God. He was strangling me and saying, 'Where's the fucking speaker, you black bastard?'

Then they picked up my mate with a truncheon between his legs. They ruptured him, really ruptured him. It was bad. It's frightening when you've got a big bastard like that with big gloves on sitting over you and strangling you and saying, 'Where's the speaker, you black bastard?' I was only thirteen.

It's violence that's made me violent.

HAVE YOU EVER REALLY LOVED ANYONE?

Yeah. The mother of my second son, I love her to bits. I absolutely love her to bits. She's so beautiful. When I used to work the doors years ago and I'd come in late, she'd be in bed. She'd sit on the end of the bed and rub my feet for me. She'd actually rub my feet while I was asleep. She'd be knackered but she'd still massage my feet. She was lovely. She and I would have our differences and I was young, a bit insecure. I screwed around with another girl and, well, there you go.

She went. Same old, same old...

WHAT FRIGHTENS YOU?

I suppose what frightens me is what revs me up. Like if a man came on to me in a funny way and I didn't know him and I was in a bar. It might intimidate me for a moment – then I retaliate with anger. I suppose it all stems from when I was younger with my father. If I'm in a difficult situation, I will make up my mind. I'm not frightened. If I have to do something, I'll go over there and do it and it's done – done my way. I don't ever want to be doing life, but I understand how easy it is to turn on someone. That's frightening.

DESCRIBE A HARD BASTARD

It's not your doorman standing there staunch with a shaven head, saying, 'I'll have yer.' That's not a problem. I'd say a hard bastard is a man who is hard from inside; he's hardened through the years. He has chosen his life and he will stand by his convictions, he will go all the way. It's not there in the exterior of a man. It's inside. It's: will he go the extra mile?

NAME A HARD BASTARD

Joey Pyle. He's staunch. He's a lovely geezer, but when Joe says it's time, it's time. All the people know that. He's got that respect from people.

WHERE DO YOU SEE YOURSELF IN FIVE YEARS?

Fuck, I hope it isn't in prison! I would like to be a millionaire, I would like to be a celebrity, I'd like to be happily married! I like the finer things in life... I don't get kicks out of doing the wrong thing but, like I said, this is a way of life and you choose it as a way of life. If I don't work, I don't get paid. I have to be professional and you learn to deal with people in a professional way because that's the way life is. I'm a people person and I get fulfilled in life by what I'm doing now.

ANY REGRETS?

Yeah, fucking that bird when I should have been with my wife. And I'd done a lot of dough for her – credit cards, champagne, hotels, diamond rings, everything. She went off with one of my mates but I could hardly complain because I nicked her from one of *my* mates! And, of course, I should have been with my wife. What goes around, comes around.

Apart from that no regrets, not really. I wrote this poem:

A thief is not a man of shame,
Merely one who advocates from blame.
He seeks the sordid life of crime
His worst nightmare is serving time
He seeks a sort of regal fame
To justify his ill-gotten gain
Heed these words I say so plain
A thief is not a man of shame.

Stevie Knock

Stevie Knock is a bouncer extraordinaire. He worked the door for thirteen years and he's seen the lot, knows the lot, had more rucks... you know the score! What Stevie doesn't know about the door isn't worth knowing!

If you're on the door, he says, you know you're going to get trouble sooner or later. If you work long enough, then you've got to be prepared. What surprised me was that he blames women for a lot of it. It's the women who often kick up, he says – 'They can start a hell of a lot.'

The women start it, then the men with them, as Stevie puts it, 'their mentality does them in. It's the old male bravado. The men finish what the women started...'

Stevie is big, bloody big. He's training and fitness mad. When he walks into a room he has a presence, an aura. Everything about him is rugged and manly. He hasn't really got a neck – it's as big as his shoulders, it's as if his head has just been plopped onto his shoulders.

Get him talking about the door and suddenly he comes alive. He has story after story of violent encounters, each one more brutal than the last. He leaps to his feet to emphasise what happened during a stabbing; he acts out every detail, not to show off or boast but to make sure I get the story exactly right. He has gone, and still would go, toe to toe with any man from here to wherever. He is as tough and brutal as they come.

But... but... every man has an Achilles' heel and Stevie is no exception.

Just the mere mention of his girlfriend's name turns this big guy to jelly. Julia is the love of his life. His girl, his sweetheart, his friend and confidante. Suddenly the conversation is no longer about violence, violence, violence. Now it's all top hat and tails, romance, bridesmaids... Yep, Stevie and Julia are getting married. Will she tame him? We'll see...

BACKGROUND

I had two sisters but one died when I was nine and she was eight. That was a big turning point for me. My other sister is still alive, she's younger than me. I was brought up in Bermondsey, we used to live down the Old Kent Road. I had a really difficult childhood. There was no money about. Dad wasn't always there so my mum brought me up alone a lot of the time. Then my sister died and that freaked me out.

I looked like a little angel but I was very, very aggressive. I think that came from looking after my sister. She was in and out of hospital for quite a while and it was me mainly looking after her. She had a malignant brain tumour so it affected her slowly; gradually it affected her speech and sight. She wore the National Health specs and, kids being kids, she was a prime target for people to have a pop at, so me and my little gang looked after her. I was leader of the gang and I was called Knock-out Knock. It was the milkman who first called me that because I used to help him, but then we fell out because I robbed him to pay for our Christmas turkey.

LIFE OF CRIME

I've been arrested numerous times but I've been lucky enough never to go away. There were accusations of violence, a few other things they couldn't prove. I've been lucky.

DO YOU THINK PRISON IS A DETERRENT?

Yes, I do, because I certainly wouldn't like my freedom taken away from me. I'm a straight guy – ish – but the trouble is when my temper gets the better of me. Normally I'm very straight, very sensible. I know what to do not to get myself into too much trouble. I try and keep two steps in front. My temper is very calculated – I can switch it on and off like a light. My trouble is – and it's a fault of me own – I tend to be too spiteful. My own attitude is that I'll always come out on top. Out of all the hundreds and hundreds of encounters, I've never lost one. Never been knocked down, never. But I've always been fair; anyone's ever hit the deck, I've never followed it up. If he goes down, he can go down and stay there and he stays there on his own.

There was an incident once when I was working the door down the Old Kent Road and I had this Portuguese guy round, telling me he was Special Forces, telling me how tough he was, this, that and the other. But then it got a bit out of hand. He told me I was too big or fat or whatever. When it actually comes to the row, I took his eye out. Because he's told me how tough he was, I've gone in all the way. I don't regret it. I've never in me life regretted anything I've done.

DO YOU BELIEVE IN CAPITAL PUNISHMENT?

I do for certain cases; the obvious one is the kids because they're defenceless so someone's got to really dish it out to these people. I couldn't actually say for all murderers because it's part and parcel.

Some people murder within their business; there are decent criminals. Definitely, it's the children really. Some women ask for it – no, that's a joke! Rapists, I don't know, what do you do with them? I think they should go with the child molesters. No man has the right to do that, to take that.

214

WHAT WOULD HAVE DETERRED YOU FROM A LIFE OF CRIME?

A very well-paid job. But to get that you'd need a good education and I haven't had the chance. Education, it's the answer to material gains. It's the answer to your everyday life – houses, cars, the way you eat, the way you go out. A good education does give you the basics.

HAVE YOU EVER BEEN STABBED/SHOT?

I've been stabbed twice in the body and cut – I had a very bad cut all around the ear. And I've been shot in the head. That happened when I was on the door. It's part of doorwork, just one of those things. It was meant for someone else but I happened to be in the way and took the full force of a shotgun. They're still in there now as reminders, there are about twenty-four shots in there.

But it's part and parcel. At the end of the day, I've dished out some, so what goes around comes around. I couldn't be a liar and a hypocrite and say I didn't do similar.

SCARIEST MOMENT?

When I was told my sister had died, it frightened the life out of me. I didn't know what I was going to do without her.

SADDEST MOMENT?

I was off on a weekend with the Cubs and my dad and my grandad met me off the minibus in the Old Kent

Road. They told me my sister had gone into hospital to have an operation for the tumour. They said she was there for the weekend but she didn't come out.

WHAT RATTLES YOUR CAGE?

Disrespect. I've got a lot of respect for people I've met, people like Roy Shaw, people that have got a history. What rattles my cage is these guys who go on and there's no proven history. They make up what they like.

I mean, if I want to talk about my past there's always been someone there to back up what I say.

So disrespect rattles my cage. And bullies. I can't stand a bully, never have done.

HAVE YOU EVER REALLY LOVED ANYONE?

My Julia – we're getting married in August. And my kids.

WHAT FRIGHTENS YOU?

Harm coming to people like my family. That's all. Not myself. Nothing bothers me like that. I'll handle it. I'm only frightened of things I can't control, when I'm not there, things happening to Julia or my family, my kids, mother, father, that sort of stuff.

DESCRIBE A HARD BASTARD

A hard bastard is someone who can have it toe to toe and always, or mainly, come out on top. He's respectful with it. He's just hard, no talk. Someone who can just get on with it, who'll row with anyone and won't pick and choose their victims.

NAME A HARD BASTARD

I think one of the toughest people I know is my mother. It's a different kind of hardness. She's tough because she's had to be, the way she coped when my sister died. She loves kids, she's so good with kids. She's had a bad time with my kids because she has difficulty seeing them as often as she'd like as my ex-wife has custody of them. That's crushing but she's tough, my mum.

Apart from that, well, I suppose I'm the toughest one I know. I've come up against all sorts and I've never shied away from a fight in my life. I just wouldn't – it's not in my nature. I would never go into a fight thinking that I was going to lose. I'm trained in the martial arts. I'm used to full-contact fighting and kick-boxing.

WHERE DO YOU SEE YOURSELF IN FIVE YEARS?

Happily married to Julia and hopefully we'll have our first child. But, still, my principles would be the same – nothing like that will change. I see myself, in five years' time, just happy really.

ANY REGRETS?

I could say about me ex but I won't. I can't have any regrets because if I had regrets I wouldn't be where I am now. So life is what it is. If I regretted things, no, maybe life could have taken a different path. I don't regret anything because things that have happened in my past have shaped my future, and have made me into the man I am today.

Daniel Reece

Danny Reece was accused, and found guilty, of murder. He's now serving life in Whitemoor Prison, Cambridgeshire.

He's also been accused of being a grass. He pleads guilty – with mitigating circumstances.

You, the reader, be the jury and decide.

On a tape he sent to me, he tried to put the record straight once and for all.

He was on a prison landing when a sixty-year-old lifer called Ronnie Easterbrook hissed, 'So you're the grass?'

It takes a brave man to stand toe to toe with Danny Reece; all the cons feared Danny. Everyone was aware when he was on the landing. Nobody approached him, or had eye contact with him, let alone insulted him by calling him a grass.

So when Ronnie Easterbrook arrived and made his accusation, everyone noticed how he didn't move out of the way or avert his eyes. Ronnie had obviously heard about Danny. His sheer size and strength made him unmistakable.

'So you're the grass?'

A breathless hush swept across the landing.

Danny later told me, 'I felt my blood boil; the palms of my hands began to sweat. I looked into the face of a sixty-year-old man who dared to call me a grass. A fucking grass! Being called a grass is the worst insult anyone can give you.

'Everyone on the landing expected me to go berserk, but I didn't – I decided to tell Ronnie Easterbrook the truth, like I'm telling you. The man involved was a murdering rapist called Dave Lashley.

'Yeah, I suppose you could call me a grass if you count taking a dirty, rotten, filthy nonce off the streets for the rest of his natural life. The way I saw it was that it could have been my mother, sister or daughter that he'd raped and murdered. I felt I had to do something.

At the time, I was in Brixton prison in south London. I was given a job in the woodmill and was allowed to train in the gym twice a week. It was there that I met Dave Lashley, a huge black man who was as strong as an ox. We worked together, trained together and had a laugh. I didn't know what Dave was in for and I didn't ask – it's not the done thing.

It was just another Tuesday morning and a screw had loaned me a copy of the *Sun*.

The headline screamed out: BLACK RAPIST JAILED FOR TEN YEARS.

Dave read the headline. 'Ten years,' he scoffed. 'He should have killed the bitch, he wouldn't have got any more time!'

I couldn't believe what I was hearing.

'The fucking rapist,' he went on. 'I killed my bitches. He raped one and got the same as me. The mug!'

For once, I was speechless. This man was a rapist, a murdering fucking rapist, and I'd been knocking about with him. Before I could say anything, Dave grabbed my head, his huge hands held my skull.

'This is how I done the bitches.' And he began to demonstrate how he killed, by pushing his fist into my windpipe. That's when I snapped. I hit him so hard it lifted him off the ground. As he flew backwards, the screws pushed the panic button but it was too late, I was on top of him. I really lost it.

By the time they pulled me off him, both of us were covered in blood. They assumed the blood was mine until they discovered a big piece of his flesh still in my mouth.

I testified against him in St Alban's Crown Court and the rapist received a natural life sentence. So yeah, I grassed – on a rapist.

Unfortunately, in prison, things are exaggerated and every time the story is told it gets bigger and bigger. I've even been accused of grassing on Linda Calvey – the woman I love, my own wife!

'What I've said here is the truth. I've put the record straight. Believe it, if you want to; if you don't, then fuck ya!'

BACKGROUND

I've lived in east London for most of my life. I was born within the sound of the Bow Bells in Mile End, Bow, which makes me a Cockney.

All I ever wanted was to be like my Uncle George. He was my boyhood hero. I never knew my dad when I was growing up – he gave my mum seven kids then fucked off. I'm the eldest of the seven – I have three sisters and three brothers. Mum did her best for us, but quite often we only just had enough to eat.

We lived in an old prefab in Manor Road, Stratford. 'The Round House' we called it – it was just like a dome with two bedrooms at the back, a small kitchen, a sitting room-cum-diner in the front and an outside toilet. There was no electricity or gas, so Mum cooked on an open fire.

Bringing up seven children obviously took its toll on Mum and she fell seriously ill. This was the early fifties. Social Services were called in and they wanted to put us into care, but Mum's sisters stepped in and the family, us kids, were split up.

I went off to live with Aunt Maud and Uncle George in Leytonstone in east London. I loved it from the start. George took me everywhere with him. He owned a scrapyard and I used to watch him throw car engines across the yard like they were cardboard boxes. I used to search cars for lost money, which I kept.

George always had time for me and I wanted to be strong and respected just like him. Maud became like a second mum to me and I loved them both.

When Mum recovered from her illness, we had to go back to the prefab. I didn't want to go – I dreaded it. I had experienced living in a proper house with gas and electric; going back to that poxy prefab was the last thing I wanted to do. I had to take drastic action. Things are simple when you're young – in my mind, if the prefab wasn't there, then the problem would be solved if we didn't have the prefab, the council would have to rehouse us in a proper house just like Uncle George and Auntie Maud. So I went berserk: smashed the windows, ripped doors off hinges, smashed down walls. I totally destroyed the prefab. I wasn't caught. My plan worked. The council were forced to rehouse us.

LIFE OF CRIME

My first court appearance, when I was young, was for criminal damage – I was caught smashing up the toilets in Stratford station.

Then there was approved school, then detention centre, then prison. Crime goes in steps. You could liken it to an apprenticeship. It starts with small-time thieving, then it progresses to bigger jobs, then the big-time, with the odd bit of malicious damage and grievous bodily harm thrown in for good measure until you reach the ultimate goal: armed robberies and murder.

I've been a criminal all my life. I've spent over twenty years in jail for armed robbery and violence. At the moment, I'm serving life for murder.

IS PRISON A DETERRENT?

No.

Prison used to be a simple place. You served your time, deprived of your freedom, living to rules and regulations that dominated your every hour. But prison today is a far cry from simple. It is full of drugs and people connected with drugs, people who live by drugs and for drugs. The drug tests are a complete waste of time and money; they achieve nothing but have created a prison system which is supposedly there to correct but, in reality, corrupts.

Heroin is expensive and very addictive. Consequently, the young kids are constantly in debt and are forced into prostitution to pay for their habit. I wish people would understand the stupidity of drugs. The only way out of any situation is to face up to it, confront it, acknowledge it – and change it.

DO YOU BELIEVE IN CAPITAL PUNISHMENT?

Child killers should be put down the same as rabid dogs.

WHAT WOULD HAVE DETERRED YOU FROM A LIFE OF CRIME?

Nothing would have stopped me from a life of crime – it was what I wanted.

HAVE YOU EVER BEEN STABBED/SHOT?
I've been stabbed five times. Shot – no.

SCARIEST MOMENT?
Watching my sons being born.

SADDEST MOMENT?
The death of my son John – it was complete hell.

WHAT RATTLES YOUR CAGE?
Petty people – and people that don't keep their promises.
In prison, you meet the very worst sort of human being
imaginable and bullies are ten-a-penny. I despise bullies;
all bullies are cowards and hide behind the fear they
instil in others. But confront a bully and he usually turns
into a coward.

HAVE YOU EVER REALLY LOVED ANYONE?
Apart from my sons and my sister's daughter, Tania, I've
loved Jennifer, my lovely wife Linda and a little Gremlin.

My future is with Linda; every day and every night I
think of her. I write to her daily. I am able to speak to
her every fortnight and, if I'm lucky, I get an hour but
sometimes it is only for ten minutes.

WHAT FRIGHTENS YOU?
No human being frightens me – I suppose love frightens
me the most.

DESCRIBE A HARD BASTARD

Someone that never gives up. Someone who believes in blood for blood and always gets his revenge.

NAME A HARD BASTARD

Ronnie Easterbrook – the only man I've given 100 per cent respect to. The Colonel and Ken Pugh.

WHERE DO YOU SEE YOURSELF IN FIVE YEARS?

I see myself lying on some exotic beach with my dream girl, counting my millions – or maybe playing in the fields of Heaven with my son John.

ANY REGRETS?

Not meeting Ronnie Easterbrook twenty years ago – what fun we would have had! And not being there to pick up my son from school.

Chris Murphy

Chris Murphy is The Quiet Man, strong, silent... He's a dangerous mother****.**

Chris became part of this book by pure accident. I'd just finished an interview with Dave Davies. Afterwards, he went one way and I went the other. An hour later, my phone rang. Dave had bumped into his old buddy, Chris Murphy, in his local off-licence. He hadn't seen him for donkey's years. Then he told me about his reputation. He is The Man, he said. I admit, I was intrigued.

I met Chris in a pub in Essex, and instantly knew what Dave meant. While he chatted, Chris smiled a lot – but never with his eyes. He never came across as mad – just slightly unhinged. I felt Chris had more depth to him than he was letting on. He was secretive about what he did and how he did it. There was something about him, something I couldn't put my finger on. After spending a couple of hours in his company, I was wiser – but not much.

What is his profession? Gangster? Security? SAS?

Whatever he is, he ain't letting on. And I ain't asking...

Well, of course I did – but decorator? Decorator, my arse!

BACKGROUND

I'm an Essex boy. I've got a younger brother and a sister. That's all I want to say about my background.

LIFE OF CRIME

I've been away. Two years, one year, I did a four-stretch for malicious intent. Violence. The last one was six months for having weapons.

DO YOU THINK PRISON IS A DETERRENT?

I don't know. To some it might be but, in general, no. It's a learning process. For youngsters, I think it might be a deterrent but when you're older, no.

DO YOU BELIEVE IN CAPITAL PUNISHMENT?

Under certain circumstances, yeah. Nonces, people like that, definitely. I'd like to fucking do it.

WHAT WOULD HAVE DETERRED YOU FROM A LIFE OF CRIME?

I don't think anything would have deterred me. Some things are meant to be. I'm not a nine-to-five person, I never could hold down a normal job. I realised that when I was about fifteen years old and helping my old man in the building trade. It was fucking hard work and I don't like that! I suppose that's why most people get into crime – why go out working hard for five or even seven days a week when you can make the same amount of money in half an hour?

So why bother?

HAVE YOU EVER BEEN STABBED/SHOT?

Yes. Both. I was shot in the leg when I was twenty. And I've been stabbed five times. The stabbings happened when I was working on the door when I was younger – the shooting was something else, something I would rather not go into. How does it feel when you're shot? It hurts! But it's strange, you know straight away you've been shot but you don't feel immediate pain, it comes on a few seconds later and you're thinking, Fuck, I've been shot. And the speed of that bullet, when it hits you, it burns you.

I've been trained in the use of most small firearms and some other weapons and I know what they can do. But we won't go into that either! I've also trained for years in the martial arts; karate and Korean martial arts. Your mind is your most dangerous weapon. I always weigh up situations – I never go into anything hot, never.

SCARIEST MOMENT?

I got stabbed when I was abroad, miles from anywhere and no one around to help. That was scary because you don't know what's coming on top at the time. I thought I was going to die... Well, I thought I was dead. I was stabbed in the back. It feels like someone's punching you, but as soon as that knife comes out, you know. If they left the fucker in there, that's all right – but when they take it out, that's what hurts.

When I was stabbed, I couldn't move and I had trouble breathing. That was scary – fighting for breath.

SADDEST MOMENT?

My wife killed herself in 1995 – and she meant to do it. We'd split up about a week before; we'd been arguing a lot, usual things. I picked up my son and took him swimming, then dropped him back. I told him to go and see where Mum was, so he went upstairs and said, 'She's asleep on the bed.' So I said, 'Don't wake her – tell her I'll come back later on, pick you up and take you for a meal and that.'

About three hours later, I called my daughter. She told me: 'Mummy's dead.'

What I didn't realise is that she was already dead when I dropped my son off. She'd already shot herself. So my son was in the house on his own with her for four hours. He was only ten at the time. He didn't have a clue because she was lying on her side with a pillow over her – she'd shot herself through the pillow. It looked like she was asleep, but she'd shot herself through the heart with one of my guns.

WHAT RATTLES YOUR CAGE?

Rudeness. I don't see any reason for rudeness in people – politeness doesn't cost you anything.

WHAT FRIGHTENS YOU?

My mum! Every time I go round there she finds me another job to do.

DESCRIBE A HARD BASTARD

Hardness comes from years – not how big you are. It all comes from up here – it's all in the mind.

NAME A HARD BASTARD

Roy Shaw. A man not to be messed with.

WHERE DO YOU SEE YOURSELF IN FIVE YEARS?

I'd like to move abroad. I'd like to live in Malta. I like the Maltese people. I'd like it if my daughter wanted to come, too, but it's up to her; she's grown up now – she's got a kiddie of her own. But that would be nice – us all together out there in the sun.

ANY REGRETS?

Yeah, getting caught! I haven't retired, as such, but let's just say I'm winding down... I think you have to realise after a certain amount of time that you aren't as young as you were, all that kind of thing. I think you realise when you're older that a lot of the things that you argued about when you were younger just aren't worth arguing about. I do think as you get older you definitely get wiser. You think about things a bit more.

What you do think about is the consequences, the repercussions of your actions as you get older. When you're young, you don't give a toss. Getting five or ten at that age – getting five or ten at my age is something entirely different, know what I mean?

When you're older, you've settled down, you've got the house and all that; you don't want to give it up. Inside, you've got three meals a day, a roof over your head... In many ways, it's worse for the people you love on the outside. Even so, I don't want to go back to that.

Geoff
Thompson

Geek, nerd, wuss...

Wrong, wrong, wrong! What you see is not always what you get.

Geoff Thompson is the most unlikely-looking hard man I've ever seen. But don't be fooled. Beneath his nylon shirt and Crimpolene slacks lies an awesome power.

You only have to read his book to know that he has been through the mill and back again.

Geoff was the only tough guy to bring me chocolates when I met him. He was chatty, witty and the perfect gent, not at all the bruiser that I'd heard about. I began to wonder if I had the right Geoff Thompson.

It made me question what a hard man is supposed to look and act like. All our preconceived ideas are of a man who can lift a ton but can't spell it! You imagine shaven heads and tattoos.

But Geoff is living proof that tough guys come in all shapes and sizes; colour, creed and age are immaterial.

It might sound sexist, but I think every man has the potential to be dangerous. Geoff Thompson is no exception, but he has used his experiences in a positive way. He has written thirty books on the subject of violence. He has written plays and film scripts, he's even published his own books. He's been there, done it.

So don't be fooled by his manner and his niceness. Someone once told me, 'Only a fool takes kindness as weakness...' That someone was Ronnie Kray.

BACKGROUND

When I was younger, I suffered from depression. I was in fear – fear of life, really. One day, I got so tired of being fearful and depressed that I thought: I've got to do something about this. So I sat down and drew a pyramid on a piece of paper. Then I wrote out all my fears, one by one. I confronted them systematically, one by one. And, at the top of the fear list was fear of violent confrontation. So I became a doorman to confront my demons. You've just got to be careful when you face the dragon that you don't become the dragon yourself. I went on the door for my own salvation, but once I was on the door, I became the dragon, hugely violent, and I started using violence, which didn't solve the problem at all.

If someone came into my world, I used violence to

knock them back out of it again. I became a person I didn't like. I changed. My mum noticed a change in me and my first wife noticed a change in me. I couldn't see it at the time – it was a gradual realisation.

People started queuing up to fight me. I was eleven-and-a-half stone, I was polite and I had the audacity to be articulate on the door; I apologised if I couldn't let anyone in – so everyone wanted to fight me. The problem was, although I was in control of the fear, I was still frightened. So if people wanted to confront me, I'd knock them out. I didn't like the feeling of the pre-fight, I didn't like the feeling of the fight itself, I only liked the feeling post-fight because the endorphins in my body were racing.

I'd have a man on the floor and I'd kick him like a coconut. It wasn't gratuitous, it was because I was frightened to death, frightened he was going to beat me because there was a part of me inside that was still a nine-stone weakling saying, 'I can't believe I've knocked him down. I'm not going to leave it so he can get up again.'

Especially the people I was dealing with – gang members and such like. It wasn't that I was brave, it was just that I didn't want him to get up and fight me again. I didn't want him to come back and fight me the next day. So, most of my violence came from insecurity.

But, as I've grown and become more confident, I've let the violence go. So I don't look at violent people and see bravery – I see insecurity. That's what martial arts does for you. I want to be so good at what I do, so confident about what I do, that I can just walk away. Even though someone might not know that I've let them off, I will let them off. Martial arts teaches you how to kill people – but once you know, there's not a single part of you that wants to do it. That's where my real strength is. I can walk away with confidence.

When you're violent, you dehumanise people – if you're kicking someone like a coconut, you can't see them as a husband or a son. They're no longer human in your eyes. But if you learn martial arts, you learn about yourself; you don't have to walk about posturing. People who really know how to take care of themselves are gentle people. I admire that and I admire intelligence.

I was in my mid-twenties when I realised. I'd suffered from anxiety, depression and fear most of my life, on and off. I realised that I wasn't really frightened of people, I was frightened of feelings. I had to live with those feelings. Now I still don't like it, but I can live with it – that comes with experience.

LIFE OF CRIME
I've never been a criminal or a gangster – I was a doorman.

DO YOU THINK PRISON IS A DETERRENT?
I don't think the present system is fantastic – I think prison should be tied in with some kind of educational programme.

Obviously you need some system which is punishment, but if we're going to send people to prison, while they're in there they should be somehow motivated and inspired to change. If people have got the skill and the bottle to make a living from crime, they can make a living from anything – they need to be shown that. It's a question of changing direction.

DO YOU BELIEVE IN CAPITAL PUNISHMENT?

No, I don't. I don't really believe in blood for blood. If someone commits a crime, they go to jail – that is the consequence of their actions. I think once you start killing people, you become them. But there's a paradox here because I would be prepared to kill somebody if my own survival was at stake.

But I wouldn't class that as violence – that's survival. If you've done everything possible in a violent confrontation to get out of the situation, but you find your own survival is at stake, that's different. You are then defending yourself. That's natural law. But capital punishment, you're killing someone in a cold-blooded way – I wouldn't want to do it, I wouldn't want to put my hand to it. I think you punish people more when you put them in prison for the rest of their lives than when you kill them.

WHAT WOULD HAVE DETERRED YOU FROM A LIFE OF CRIME?

It was a growing realisation that violence doesn't work – so I started to try not to be violent. So, when I was working the doors, I tried to solve all the problems by communicating, by talking. It didn't always work.

There was one particular guy who was trouble, but I tried to talk him down. Unfortunately, he mistook my politeness for weakness and over three months he just got more and more rude. We ended up having a fight in the car park. I knocked him down, first punch, but I was so angry; all the anger of the previous three months came out and I just destroyed him. I couldn't control my anger. I thought I'd killed him – I hadn't – but in my mind I had. Everybody gathered round and there were people saying, 'He's dead, he's dead.' They took him off to hospital and I remember driving home; it was a lonely drive home. I kept thinking, I'm going to go to prison.

I got home and my wife was in bed asleep and the kids were asleep and I looked at them and they were so beautiful. It was as if a veil dropped from my eyes; it was like a film and I thought, I'm losing her, I'm losing them and for what?

So I stopped working on the door and I started writing books. That was the turning point for me. I just realised that I was risking so much by behaving as I was.

HAVE YOU EVER BEEN STABBED/SHOT?

I got slashed about half a dozen times when I was working at a club in Coventry – but that was a big gang fight. A whole gang of them came in on a stag night and the whole place exploded; it got destroyed, glass everywhere – there was about three thousand pounds'-worth of broken glass. I got wounds in my head and in my hands. I went down, but I kept getting up. But if I'd gone down and stayed down, I think I would have died that night.

SCARIEST MOMENT?

That fight I had with the guy in the car park. That was my scariest moment. It wasn't that I was afraid of being hurt. I was more scared of losing my liberty, my wife and kids. Physical hurt you can deal with, it's the internal hurt that's worse.

SADDEST MOMENT?

Losing my first wife and kids. My first wife was a good girl but we got married when we were seventeen and as we grew up, we became two different people. Then, after we split up, I was in social Siberia – I was in a bedsit and that's all I had, the bedsit. That was the hardest time. I love my kids and I'd always been with them. Leaving the marital home was the hardest thing I ever did. I don't regret it. I had to do it. But it was hard.

WHAT RATTLES YOUR CAGE?

Prejudice. I love colours, I love the different cultures, I love the diversity. I don't like people who judge other people just on the grounds of colour or whatever. I don't think any of us have got the right to judge other people like that.

HAVE YOU EVER REALLY LOVED ANYONE?

Yeah, the lady I'm with now – Sharon. She's my whole life. I love her so much I can't tell you. I can write it down but I can't get it out. She's my soul-mate and I love her so very much. When I met her, I had such an overwhelming feeling of love and I think that's what God must be – that feeling. I don't see God as an old man with a beard, I see God as every living thing, I see God as love, I see God as that feeling.

DESCRIBE A HARD BASTARD

My description of a hard bastard isn't very nice. A hard bastard isn't someone who can just have a fight; a hard bastard is someone that is hard through and through. He's hard with his kids, he's hard with his wife, he's hard with everybody. If I had to describe it in one word, I'd say it was someone who was unhappy. It's not someone I want to be. If someone said I was a hard bastard, I'd feel I had failed. Being hard isn't good. Hardiness is good, by which I mean you can cope with pain.

NAME A HARD BASTARD

Some of the characters in Charles Dickens' books are hard bastards. Scrooge was a hard bastard. He was hated – hard bastards are hated.

WHERE DO YOU SEE YOURSELF IN FIVE YEARS?

I see myself as a West End playwright with my own film showing at a nearby cinema. I see myself happy with my wife and my kids working for me in my publishing company. I see myself really happy in five years.

ANY REGRETS?

I can't regret anything. I'm the living manifestation of everything that's ever happened to me and if I changed anything now I wouldn't be the person I am now.

I wish I hadn't hurt people, but if I hadn't hurt people no one would listen to me now when I say don't hurt people. So no, no regrets.

Dave Davis

Early evening in an Essex pub. Dave Davis – D to his friends – is leaning on the bar. It's his round. Holding a crisp fifty-pound note, he asks with a nod, 'What yer 'avin?'

He is thirty-six years old, broadly built, dressed in a navy suit, a no-nonsense, upfront, in-your-face kinda guy.

He handed me my drink without looking at me. In fact, throughout the interview, he hardly glanced in my direction. If he wasn't talking out of the corner of his mouth on his mobile phone, then he was acknowledging shifty-looking characters with a nod.

Dave Davis is a man's man. That's obvious. He's also one of those men in a hurry – things to do, people to see, places to go. He keeps his cards close to his chest, he gives little away. He was very careful about what he said – and how he said it. A man of few words.

'Don't say much, do you?' I said.

He smiled and, for the first time, looked at me, really looked at me. His blue eyes went straight through me and he whispered, 'Why use two words when one will do?'

But then he started to talk...

BACKGROUND

I've spent most of my life in Essex. My uncle is Davey Hunt, a well-respected man in Essex. I've got a brother and a sister.

I was a bit of a rogue when I was growing up – I couldn't take authority very well, school and all that, I just didn't like being there. I didn't get on with the other kids that well.

LIFE OF CRIME

I've done time – for violence. I served two out of four when I was nineteen. That gave me a quick shock and I haven't been back since.

IS PRISON A DETERRENT?

No, not really. Because if you're going to do it, you're going to do it anyway. If you start thinking about things, it's going to hurt you rather than just getting on and doing it. Now I'm older, prison is more of a deterrent, but when I was younger, no, it wasn't. It's not so much your age, it's when you've got kids of your own – you've got to think of them. They slow you down. Who's going to get them their bread and butter? It makes you more sensible.

DO YOU BELIEVE IN CAPITAL PUNISHMENT?

Mainly no, but for child rapes, all that kind of thing, it goes without saying, doesn't it? Yes.

WHAT WOULD HAVE DETERRED YOU FROM A LIFE OF CRIME?

Lots of money, having wealthy parents. I wouldn't get up and do what I do every day if I had loads of money to burn.

HAVE YOU EVER BEEN STABBED/SHOT?

Yeah, I've been cut, stabbed and I've been shot.

SCARIEST MOMENT?

I haven't really had a scary moment – they come afterwards when you think back on what's happened and you think, That was a bit lively.

In fact, the scariest moment really was when my kids were born; I could hardly stay in the same hospital. I went white and I was having panic attacks. I was frightened, I had to go.

Then I came back when the baby was born and then I had to go again. Now I've got three little girls and a boy – he's only seven months. I didn't see any of them being born – I just couldn't. Seeing a woman in labour with your child is the scariest thing in the world.

SADDEST MOMENT?

I lost my dad about five weeks ago. My saddest moment ever – still playing on me now. It was a brain tumour. He was only fifty. He was governor round this manor. It's been a terrible, terrible shock.

He complained of headaches for three days, went to work, fell asleep in the cab of a lorry and never woke up again. I don't think I will ever get over his death. He wasn't just my dad – he was my best mate. I'm devastated.

WHAT RATTLES YOUR CAGE?

West Ham upset me! But, seriously, paedophiles, people who don't treat their kids right – that really upsets me. Nothing much else.

HAVE YOU EVER REALLY LOVED ANYONE?

My mum and dad. My kids. I don't feel the same for any woman as I feel when I hold my beautiful daughters in my arms or my baby boy. I've never felt such love as the love I feel for them.

DESCRIBE A HARD BASTARD

A hard bastard is a man who's fearless. He doesn't have to be a hard bastard as such – just fearless, scared of nothing.

NAME A HARD BASTARD

My mother, Stephanie. She's fearless.

WHERE DO YOU SEE YOURSELF IN FIVE YEARS?

I can see us in a little house – out of the way so no one could find me, out in the sticks somewhere, comfortably off, retired – but I suppose I've retired already! I've done the door since I was seventeen but I've stopped doing it now, so that's retirement.

ANY REGRETS?

No. If a man regrets his past, then he regrets his life. So, no, I've no regrets.

Jamie O'Keefe

'Personally, I would be a very happy man if I never get into another fight in my life. It really pisses me off when someone forces me along the path of violence, but I am also not able to turn the other cheek and find forgiveness.

'If somebody hurts a member of my family, I would not think twice about unleashing every nasty form of painful application that I know of. Don't get me wrong – I'm not a monster. If you spill my beer in a pub, I would not consider that to be something worth fighting for.

'If you road rage me, I still do not consider it something worth fighting for. However, change the scenario and road rage me while I have children in the car, then I would not hesitate to come tearing through your street door at 5.00 a.m. and break every bone in your body before you even wipe the sleep from your eyes. I've done that a few times when it was deserved...'

So writes Jamie O'Keefe in his book, *Thugs, Mugs*

and Violence. 'Forget the movies, this is the real world' it says on the cover.

Jamie is a man of words, the author of numerous books on self-protection. Apart from *Thugs*, he's written *Old School, New School – A Guide to Bouncers*. Then there's *Dogs Don't Know Kung-Fu*, a female guide to self-protection and *Pre-emptive Strikes for Winning Fights*, the alternative to 'grappling'.

What makes Jamie unusual is that he has published them all himself. And I've got to take my hat off to him. If there was an award for trying, then Jamie wins it hands down. He knows what he's talking about, too. A former doorman through the late seventies, the eighties and nineties, he's living proof that not all doormen are meatheads.

Yes, Jamie can lift a ton – and spell it. Power to you, Jamie. Go, Jamie, go!

BACKGROUND

These days, I work with young kids – help them to try and get back on track. When I was about eight years old, a close family member was sexually abused by my dad and I was told about it. You just imagine what it's like dealing with all that information at that age, knowing your dad's a nonce.

So I set fire to our house, which was on an estate in Bethnal Green. I was confused. The house felt unclean and I didn't know what to do with it because of my dad.

I burnt the house down. Then the police got involved and my dad got sent down for what he did. Me and my sister got sent to Scotland to live with our nan, for safety's sake. Then we came back and lived in Dagenham and started life again. Then my mum got involved with someone else and he became my stepfather. I've never seen my real father since the day I set fire to the house.

LIFE OF CRIME

None. The nearest I got to it was when the police paid me a visit when Frank Warren, the promoter, got shot. I was training the guy who allegedly shot him, but who was rightly acquitted. Also, I was a legally licensed firearms holder, but they quickly found out my guns weren't connected in any way. No, even working the door I've never been prosecuted for anything or been sent away.

IS PRISON A DETERRENT?

It depends on what sort of crime you were thinking of committing. I think most people who are committing robberies think they're going to get away with it. For them, prison is no deterrent. I don't think prison is a deterrent to people like paedophiles either, because they don't think they're doing wrong. I think if you've committed just one crime and you go to prison, you probably end up learning more inside than you would outside on the street. So, it doesn't really seem to work, does it?

DO YOU BELIEVE IN CAPITAL PUNISHMENT?

I do believe in capital punishment, but it does worry me that there are sometimes miscarriages of justice and it all goes wrong. Even so, I think there should be capital punishment for sexually related crimes, paedophiles and rape. For murder, it depends so much on the circumstances. I have a friend doing life for murder – he stabbed someone – but that really was in self-defence. This guy, he's lost his life, the young guy lost his life, all in the space of a few seconds.

I think capital punishment should be there, each judged on the facts of the case, and it should be by lethal injection. I don't believe in hanging. That's gory. It makes us as bad as them to watch someone suffering.

WHAT HAS DETERRED YOU FROM A LIFE OF CRIME?

My stepfather, who brought me up, was into crime all the time. We used to have to go to visit him in prison. He did all sorts and if I'd followed him, I would have gone down. But because he used to beat me up when I was a kid, I didn't get that close to him. He also used to beat my mum up; he used to beat the shit out of her and because I was a skinny little kid I couldn't do anything much about it. So I learnt martial arts. I wanted to build myself up so I could kill him. That was the intention – I mean, I used to watch him smash her head against the mantelpiece. This was when I was about ten until I was fifteen.

So I started judo when I was about twelve and went

on from there to karate, kick-boxing and kung fu. Then, as I became stronger, he became weaker and more frail and he knew I could have bashed him if I'd wanted to. At the same time, I had in a strange way become attached to him – when he died when I was in my thirties I cried my eyes out.

In his last year, he was in a wheelchair and he wasn't able to hurt anybody, he was that ill. It was terrible what he did to my mum and they were divorced at the end, but without that upbringing I wouldn't have learnt all I did and I wouldn't have gone into martial arts so, in a funny way, he helped me … he kept me from following him into crime.

The upbringing he gave me moulded me, it made me streetwise.

HAVE YOU EVER BEEN STABBED/SHOT?

I've been stabbed three times and cut. It was at a club in Canning Town – I've also been shot at by another doorman in my own garden with my own gun! We had a disagreement. He was into drugs and I'm not into drugs; he let me down one night on the door and I got badly beaten up. He came round my house to sort things out and guns and knives and things were out at the time. He raised one of my guns to my head in the garden and pulled the trigger. It was empty, but … after that I got rid of my guns.

SCARIEST MOMENT?

It was when I was at a club. Four or five men got my head down on the pavement and caved my face in, and then threw me over the bridge where the railway lines are. At the time I was petrified. There wasn't much I could do. Two held me down, one stamped on my face and the others were holding my legs.

SADDEST MOMENT?

When my mum died last September. Also my divorce. Losing the kids. That was sheer hell.

WHAT RATTLES YOUR CAGE?

Anyone harming weak people. I hate to see injustice being done.

HAVE YOU EVER REALLY LOVED ANYONE?

Yes, once. She knows who she is.

DESCRIBE A HARD BASTARD

A hard bastard is someone, male or female, who can go through a real drama and come out the other side, dust themselves down, and carry on. Pure physical strength alone doesn't make you a hard bastard.

NAME A HARD BASTARD

In every street, in every town, there are hard bastards. People whose name you wouldn't know – you just pass them in the street. Most of them are unknown.

WHERE DO YOU SEE YOURSELF IN FIVE YEARS?

Writing bestsellers – just like you!

ANY REGRETS?

There are some people I would have liked to have dealt with when my mum was alive rather than now she's dead. Then she would have known that I dealt with them. That's the only regret I have.

I don't want to be seen as a tough guy. I don't want to hurt anybody. My little girl was at school and the teacher asked the kids to say what their mums and dads did for a living. My little girl said, 'My dad's a bumper.' So the teacher asked her what she meant. My daughter explained, 'He throws people out of clubs and beats them up.'

'Oh,' said the teacher. 'You mean a bouncer.'

But that's how my little girl saw me and I regret that. I don't want people to think of me like that. I want the kids I work with to think I'm a nice person and to respect me as someone who works hard. If I touch people's lives, I want to touch them in a positive way.

Marco

Marco is a Hells Angel – and that means a lot. He runs a pub – named Goodfellows after the gangster film – and you know you've got the right place because Marco's Harley-Davidson is parked right outside and inside his Hells Angels of England jacket, with colours, is lying on a table.

I did a bit of research about the Hells Angels before I met Marco because I know little about them and, like a lot of other people I suppose, I have this picture in my head of men with big beards, long, grubby hair, perhaps holding a bottle of Jack Daniel's in one hand and, of course, wearing the well-worn leather jacket with skull and crossbones.

Well, I was right about the jacket. But as for my idea of bikers surrounded by snakes and naked ladies – forget it!

The Hells Angels live by a code of honour and silence. I knew Marco wouldn't let me into too many secrets, so

I had to ask around. What I found out was astonishing – the Hells Angels are the fastest-growing criminal (some would say) organisation in the world.

They earn money – big money. The organisation is made up of different clubs all over the world. America is big on Hells Angels, but Europe is rapidly becoming big, too. Yet here, in the UK, I was told there are only about twelve genuine Hells Angels clubs with between twenty members to just five or six in each – that's just two hundred true Hells Angels. And, at the moment, there are a lot of 'wars', fierce rivalries in which people are actually getting killed.

So, there aren't many genuine Hells Angels – although there are obviously a lot of wannabes – because getting into what is really a brotherhood is no easy matter. Being a Hells Angel is a total lifestyle. There are a lot of parties but a lot of jealousies, too, especially when a new member comes in and wants to make a reputation for himself.

To become a member of the club, first you have got to convince the other members about who you are, about your honesty and integrity, because to its members and to others, it is a very prestigious club. It takes a lot to get in but not much to be thrown out – lying is one thing that will get you out real quick – and a good beating to go with it. If you are caught thieving from another member, it will cost you everything: it will ruin your life.

To get in, someone usually shows an interest by simply turning up to drink wherever the Angels are drinking.

There's a 'hanging around' period of about a year. Then there's a year of what the Angels call 'prospecting', when you get Hells Angels on the back of your jacket, the Death's head and the name of your club. Next, you might become a sergeant, making sure everyone is 'taken care of' – whatever that means – and you have to prove your worth and worthiness. If you're up to it and if you get a 100 per cent 'yes' vote from your club, you get in.

And once you're in, you're accepted by Hells Angels all over the world. Hells Angels do business in Africa, America, Australia and, wherever they travel, they never have to take cash – apparently, you just get off a plane, ring a contact and they will fix you up with accommodation, money and, of course, transport!

It all sounded very impressive, albeit in a bit of a scary way. So driving over to Marco's pub, I felt a bit apprehensive. Getting an interview with this genuine Hells Angel for this book had been hard – harder than getting Johnny Adair, the terrorist; harder than getting the gangsters; harder than getting the Triads.

The reason is simple – they all stick together. They have to go in front of a 'board' and have every other member's seal of approval before they agree to talk to you, or they're not allowed to talk.

In the event the pub turned out to be smashing – just a normal, very nice pub. Marco was intelligent, charming, witty, and quite flattering in the things he said to me. The first thing I noticed when we met was his jewellery – lots of it and lots of Death's heads – closely followed by his piercing blue eyes which momentarily met mine. There was no grubby long hair, no beard – he was strikingly neat and tidy – and the Jack Daniel's was behind the bar.

But his neatness was offset by an unmistakable whiff of raw power. You can see in his eyes if he likes you... But if he doesn't ...

BACKGROUND

I'm half-Italian. I was brought up in east London – Peckham, Barking, Whitechapel. When I worked in a club, they called me a Cockney Wop.

It wasn't what you'd call a normal childhood, I suppose – I was brought up in children's homes, then Borstal, then prison. There were seven of us in my family – four sisters and three brothers. I was second down, second eldest.

LIFE OF CRIME

A little bit. I've been in prison for affray, armed robbery – kids stuff. I've done four years all told.

IS PRISON A DETERRENT?

No. You're the only deterrent, it's up to you – prison is just something you get on top. Age doesn't deter you either. I think the older you get, the wilder you should get. You don't want to end up in a hospice somewhere. Why do you want to calm down as you get older? If you calm down, you die.

DO YOU BELIEVE IN CAPITAL PUNISHMENT?

No. I don't think it deters anyone from anything. If you're going to kill someone, you're going to kill them. You're not going to sit there thinking about it, about what's going to happen to you.

WHAT WOULD HAVE DETERRED YOU FROM
A LIFE OF CRIME?

I haven't had a life of crime – but nothing would deter you. I believe you've got to live your life the way you want to live it and don't let anything deter you from that because otherwise you spend your life regretting it.

HAVE YOU EVER BEEN STABBED/SHOT?

Neither. I've been shot at – but never shot.

SCARIEST MOMENT?

I think going out with a girl for the first time was the scariest.

SADDEST MOMENT?

Getting dumped by the girl!

WHAT RATTLES YOUR CAGE?

Bullshit pisses me off. People who try to impress you, name-droppers, all that. People who try to get round you, who fake friendship.

HAVE YOU EVER REALLY LOVED ANYONE?

Yes. Once. I believe you only ever really love once. I don't think you know when you're in love – you only know it when you've lost it. But it's definitely true that it's better to have loved and lost than never to have loved at all.

WHAT FRIGHTENS YOU?

Living too long. Living too long and not being capable of doing things for yourself. I'd hate to have to be looked after, walking around with a Zimmer frame, walking up the road talking to yourself and swearing at people, all that kind of thing.

DESCRIBE A HARD BASTARD

A Smith & Wesson.

NAME A HARD BASTARD

A Glock.

WHERE DO YOU SEE YOURSELF IN FIVE YEARS?

Exactly what I'm doing now. Being a Hells Angel. I enjoy my life. Being a Hells Angel is being a total, honest, genuine person to another brother, a club member. There's nothing you wouldn't do for that person, you'd go to jail for that person, you'd die for that person if you had to.

To me, if you've got a friend, you'd do anything for that friend and you expect that back. There's no excuses.

What we've got is, I think, what a lot of people want – they want to know that if something happens to them, their family would be looked after not just for a while but for years, if necessary. To become a Hells Angel you have to be over twenty-one, be a male, have a Harley-Davidson and have it in your heart to become a Hells Angel and live by the code. It takes about two or three years. You only wear colours when you become a full member.

I've been a Hells Angel since I was eighteen – they've changed the age now to twenty-one – but I joined when I was eighteen. The Hells Angels have conquered more countries than any other force in history. There are Hells Angels everywhere. We're not all the same, we're all individuals. We don't all like rock music. But we've all got one thing in common – we all want to keep our independence. We're a democracy. If anything has to be decided, the majority rules. If you want to do something – like this interview – you go to a meeting. It's discussed, a vote is taken and then you abide by that.

If the vote had gone that I shouldn't talk to you for this book I would have abided by that.

ANY REGRETS?
No. I'd do it all again.

Kalvinder
Dhesi

Kalvinder – or Kal as everyone knows him – has a fearsome tattoo of two crossed swords. This marks the fact that he is a Sikh warrior.

Kal is a big, powerful Asian man and he's proud to be Asian. He's also proud to be a Sikh. And he's also one hard man.

Kal is well known within Asian communities. Inevitably the Asian community has its own clubs, its own gangs and its own tough guys to control those clubs. Kal is a troubleshooter for a lot of Asian clubs in the South-East.

Being Asian, Kal has had to put up with his share of racism. His smashing girlfriend, the mother of his children, is white so she gets it, too.

I loathe racism – my mother is mixed-race so I grew up witnessing racial hatred and I understood what they were talking about. But I was shocked when Kal's wife talked to me about her experiences. She told me that older Asians had spat at her and Kal in their own home town when their youngest was a baby.

'The baby was crying so Kal picked him up and people kept looking at us,' she said. 'Because the baby is quite light-skinned, they couldn't imagine what Kal was doing picking up this baby. Most people are OK, but I do think the older generation have a problem with mixed-race relationships and families.

'All Kal's friends have been brilliant – they've never looked at us differently, but when my first baby was very young I do remember someone looking in the pram and saying, "Look at that black baby there." I've never forgotten that and I never will.'

Kal and his family live in a huge, flash house with electric gates and a Mercedes in the drive on the outskirts of Kent. He was nervous when he met me and a little bit suspicious. Everything about him was big – the house, the car, even his hands, and he shook mine with a vice-like grip.

But he was very polite and very softly spoken. He had eyes like crushed black velvet ... an interesting man, I think, and, maybe, a dangerous one.

BACKGROUND

I've worked on doors for the last twelve years. It wasn't something I set out to do but I got the job because of my reputation; it came along, I took it and, twelve years later, I'm still doing it.

I was born in Plumstead. My mum and dad were from India originally. I'm the second of three brothers. We're three very different characters. I suppose I'm what you might call the black sheep of the family. I'm divorced and I've got four kids – two from my marriage and two from a previous relationship. If any of my kids ever wanted to do door work, I'd have a serious talk with them, a very serious talk.

LIFE OF CRIME

I've been in prison but it was a short sentence – twenty-eight days. I was done for possession of firearms, cannabis and stolen goods. It was all around the time of the firearms amnesty in the late eighties. I had a shotgun and didn't hand it in and someone grassed on me.

IS PRISON A DETERRENT?

No. Inside you meet other inmates who are into other things, you learn things. Basically it's an education for criminals.

DO YOU BELIEVE IN CAPITAL PUNISHMENT?

Yes, for child molesters and paedophiles. Personally, I think they should be tortured first; they should go through mental and physical hell. Straightforward capital punishment is too easy for them.

WHAT WOULD HAVE DETERRED YOU FROM A LIFE OF CRIME?

Nothing.

HAVE YOU EVER BEEN STABBED/SHOT?

No.

SCARIEST MOMENT?

I don't know. I can't think of any scary moments.

SADDEST MOMENT?

When me mum and me nan passed away. My mum passed away four years ago and my nan just recently.

WHAT RATTLES YOUR CAGE?

Racism. Racist abuse. I used to get a lot of it when I first started on the door at Rochester after I'd turned people away, I endured a lot of comments. I used to snap, but I've accepted it now. I ignore it. But then sometimes I can snap just like that because I don't see why you should get treated like that because of your colour.

If I turn someone away from the door, it isn't because of their colour; there's always a valid reason. Other doormen – white doormen – don't get that abuse, so why should I? I have been arrested a few times when I've retaliated. When I'm not working I get it, too, and – especially if I'm with the kids – I don't retaliate. I just ignore it and walk on.

I do think things have improved in Britain since the early eighties. It's better now than it used to be. People are more tolerant. And I don't think it depends on whether you live North or South. It all depends on what the situation is like where you are – unemployment, housing, things like that. I've worked the door on Asian clubs and sometimes I've had more trouble there than in mixed clubs! Then there's the problems of caste, religion ... all that. But here in Rochester I get respect from Asian people and no trouble from local people and if they've got any grief, I'll try and sort it out.

HAVE YOU EVER REALLY LOVED ANYONE?

Yes. My girlfriend.

WHAT FRIGHTENS YOU?

Anything to do with my kids being hurt. That frightens me. I was with my son a few years ago in the park and he fell into a pool. I grabbed his arm and he was OK but I was in a state, I was sweating all day. I felt so utterly helpless, sick.

DESCRIBE A HARD BASTARD

Someone who is fair and firm and who can deal with complications without going out and getting guns. Someone who can assess a situation and deal with it nicely, verbally, always firm and fair. If it comes to it – then fair enough. But a hard bastard can make someone walk away from a fight. There's nothing wrong with swallowing your pride and walking away from a fight that's unnecessary.

NAME A HARD BASTARD
Roy Shaw.

WHERE DO YOU SEE YOURSELF IN FIVE YEARS?
I haven't thought about it. Maybe still doing the door – but who knows?

ANY REGRETS?
None whatsoever.

Lou Yates

Ferrets, whippets, flat caps and coal ... and some nasty bastards.

That's it. I know they're clichés, but that's about all I know about north of the border – north of the border being anywhere past the Watford Gap! Get me north of Watford and I'm lost!

But I wanted to include some Northern hard men in this book, so I started ringing around and asking well-known tough guys. There's Charlie Seiga, of course. And quite a few others. But one name kept cropping up time and time again – 'Wild Thing'.

'Wild Thing?' I kept asking.

'Wild Thing – you know, Lou Yates.'

I didn't, but I soon found out. Some said he was the best doorman, not just up North, but in London, too.

Nah, I thought, I can't believe that.

Others said he was a champion bare-knuckle fighter

in the seventies – even going up against the likes of Pretty Boy Shaw.

Nah, didn't believe that either.

The two things everyone agreed on was his size – he's as big as a semi-detached – and his jolly sense of humour.

Well, I just had to track this happy monster down and find out for myself. It took two days of ringing around and – Bingo! – I was on my way to a meeting. And from the moment we met, Wild Thing and I got on like a house on fire.

It didn't matter how many ferret or whippet snipes I made to Lou, he'd just throw back his head and laugh. Then he'd come back with a few quips about Nancy Southerners – quite right, too!

And that's how it's been every time we talk – and we talk often, because Lou does love a chat. When he rings, I know I'm going to be on the phone for an hour, a good hour, not talking about anything in particular, just laughing and listening to Lou laughing raucously.

Lou wants to write about his life. If he does, one thing is for sure; there will be plenty of words, plenty of laughs, thoughts, happiness – and plenty of sadness too.

Lou has been through it all and come out laughing, and that's no bad thing. Perhaps we can all learn a thing or two from Lou and from his experiences. I know I have – ferrets bite!

LOU YATES

BACKGROUND

I was brought up in Lancashire – we were just a normal, average family. I've got one brother and two sisters – I don't have anything to do with them now. I was a little bastard when I was growing up. I wouldn't say I found trouble or trouble found me – it was 50–50.

I think I've always fought because my mother used to say to me, 'Why do you always talk with your fists?' I used to say to my mother, 'The reason I talk with my fists is that every bastard understands it.' I'm the same now. It's a universal language, isn't it?

I was eighteen when I started working the door. I'd been kicked out – not literally – from this club, the best one in town. Even The Beatles played there once in the early days. At Christmas I went back to go in again. I got called over and I thought, Oh God, they're going to kick me out again.

Instead, the owner said, 'Do you want to work over Christmas? Work with us. We need some extra men. If you're interested, see the manager in the office.'

And that was that. That's how I started. I was training hard, I never used to drink but I trained a lot. Train, train, train all the time. But the first night on the door, a couple of the bouncers took me up the road to a pub for a drink in the early evening before the club opened. I had a couple of Scotches and I was gone, because I never used to drink. I learnt a lot very quickly! It was a great challenge.

People knew I was a boxer – my name had been in

the papers – and there were these thirty-year-olds I had to take care of. I was only a lad. It was a challenge all right and one I relished. It set the pattern for my adult life.

LIFE OF CRIME

Nothing heavy. I've never been in prison. I've been very, very lucky. I have been arrested lots of times – always violence, and always innocent. Of course!

DO YOU THINK PRISON IS A DETERRENT?

To a degree – but not for everyone, no. A lot of people just come out and do it again. Well, you learn more in there, don't you? You meet mates in there and, when you come out, it just snowballs.

DO YOU BELIEVE IN CAPITAL PUNISHMENT?

I don't know. When I was a child, when I was younger, my uncle was birched. When he died of lung cancer, when he was sixty or whatever, he still had those marks on his back. He was only a kid. That was all wrong. It didn't do anything to change things. So capital punishment, I really don't know...

WHAT WOULD HAVE DETERRED YOU FROM A LIFE OF CRIME?

I haven't had a life of crime as such, but if I'd lived in London, I would have been very involved in it, definitely. The excitement of it. But where I came from, there wasn't that much, not like the people down South. I was a Northern bastard!

HAVE YOU EVER BEEN STABBED/SHOT?

I've been stabbed twice. Once in the back and once in the arm – both times working the doors. The strange thing about being stabbed is, at the time, you don't know at all, you don't feel it right then – you feel it afterwards, you feel the wetness of the blood.

When I was stabbed, I didn't know at all. I'd finished work in Barking – I'd had to fight off about fifteen roughnecks that night. It was one of those nights. When I finished work, I used to call into a pub on my way home and my friend who ran it used to pay me to help him close up and get rid of the people who wouldn't leave. I went in there after I'd been stabbed and I didn't even realise I'd been stabbed. I met my wife in there and I took my jacket off and she said, 'You've got blood all over your back.' They looked and there was a wound at the base of the spine about an inch-and-a-half deep.

I looked in a mirror and the blood was just pumping out. The medics said if it had been an inch further over, I'd probably have been paralysed. But it wasn't. I was OK.

Have I been shot at? Oh yes, more than once. Of course more than once! You work the doors, you expect it. But there have been so many incidents over the years, I forget them.

SCARIEST MOMENT?

To be honest, no bullshitting, I don't really get frightened about things. I remember one man pulling a shooter on me when I was on the door and saying, 'You're going to die, you bastard!' I said, 'Well, go on then, fucking kill me. Go on, shoot me.'

I said it three times. I knew then that he wasn't going to shoot me. He was a young lad, he'd been in the Army in Northern Ireland so he knew what he was doing. I watched him pull the gun and load the magazine. But he didn't want to shoot me, not really. I told him just to put the gun in his pocket. I started to walk towards him saying, 'You can frighten people with that. Just put it in your pocket and go.'

He said, 'You're not going to try anything, are you?'

I said, 'No.' In fact, I just wanted to get close to him. In a flash, I saw my chance, grabbed hold of him, got the gun out of his pocket and hit him over the head with it. He went down immediately. I took him round the corner and dumped him there. The bloke from the kebab shop called the Old Bill and about twelve of them arrived with guns. But it was all sorted out. I explained what had happened and said I didn't want him nicked. The lad now calls me a mate. But that was a bit scary at the time.

SADDEST MOMENT?

When my mum and dad died. My dad died of heart problems in his seventies and I think Mum died in sympathy a while later. I think she wished herself to death after Dad died. After he went that's all she talked about – 'I want to die to be with Dad.'

WHAT RATTLES YOUR CAGE?
Mouthy bastards, loud people.

HAVE YOU EVER REALLY LOVED ANYONE?
My kids. My mum, although I used to get beatings from her. My dad used to do it on instructions from my mother. I loved her but she had a terrible, terrible temper.

WHAT FRIGHTENS YOU?
Not violence, violence doesn't frighten me at all, because I've never lost a street fight since I left school. All the clubs I've worked – I've never come unstuck. I think now, at my age, I think falling in love with someone would frighten me.

DESCRIBE A HARD BASTARD
A hard bastard has got to be hard physically and hard mentally. A real hard bastard has got to be both.

NAME A HARD BASTARD
Roy Shaw.

WHERE DO YOU SEE YOURSELF IN FIVE YEARS?
Prison, maybe.

There are people who have betrayed me and I wake up morning after morning thinking I might just do them all – and I just might.

ANY REGRETS?

Yes. I regret never going to America when I was boxing. My life would have been very different then. I would have done well in America when I was younger if I hadn't got married early. All that.

Duchy Peter

Duchy wears extraordinary gold jewellery – one piece is a man's gold tooth, a molar on a chain. He ripped it out of a geezer's mouth after a fight.

Un-fucking-believable – that's the only word I can think of to describe Duchy. He is just that.

I'd heard of this man who was a mean mother******* who had been nicked for this and that, who'd worked the doors – apparently, he was a musician, bouncer, fighter, tough guy, black, charismatic, great talker ... and as if that wasn't enough, he was a victim of thalidomide as a child, and has no legs.

Like I said, un-fucking-believable! It's easy to be patronising about disabled people and, I must admit, when I first went to see Duchy, all the stereotypes ran through my mind. I hadn't been in his flat long before I realised that I was the disabled person – I couldn't do half the things that Duchy does and I've got both my pins.

Here is a man who has been dealt a poxy hand in life, but he has jumped up, grabbed life by the neck, shook the living daylights out of it and then some. Duchy is an inspiration. I'm not just saying that because of his disability but because of the way he has handled – and continues to handle – what's been thrown at him; he has no legs, he has a disabled sister, he had a miserable childhood, he was put into care, he's been in prison, and his wife left him to bring up their children on his own. Shall I go on?

That's enough to bring anyone to their knees (sorry, Duchy!).

He's just taken on a new door job in south-east London. He's incredibly fit, weightlifts, works out, plays golf, and he's a karate black belt.

He's also a very interesting, if introspective, man.

I think when God has to dish out the crappy things in his medical box, he dishes it out to people who he knows are strong enough to cope. Duchy is one of those. I'm glad I met him.

BACKGROUND

I was born in Lewisham, south London. I was brought up in Limehouse and went to a school for the physically disabled, which I shouldn't have done because I was the only able-bodied person there. I was fostered from an early age – I didn't go back to my parents until later on.

It wasn't an easy upbringing; it was hard, complicated. I went from children's home to children's home. Then I got totally uncontrollable and got packed off to east London, where I learnt to be naughty!

I haven't always been a fighter. I used to be a real coward but then I got really fed up with getting hit. I suddenly realised that if you barked at the world, it jumped – you know what I mean. Think about it. If the world barks at you, you jump, don't you? If you bark back, it makes life a little bit easier.

Perhaps at heart I was always a fighter because you've got to be a fighter to live with the disability I've got and be able to deal with it. Now I've come to the conclusion that I'm always going to be fighting, whether it's British Telecom or the Council or the big old geezer up the road who parks his van on the corner so I can't get my wheelchair past. I'm always going to be a fighter but I have to be. That's my life now and I've accepted that. To live with this disability day to day you must be a fighter. I've obviously thought a lot about my disability, God, all that. I do agree that God gives disabilities to strong people.

I also believe that he gives you this disability to slow you down a bit because I don't know what I would have been like without this disability. I've had my friends say that to me – I would have been a horrible this or that! As it is, I like the person I am, I really do.

There was a time when I didn't like myself when the old skulduggery slipped in, but I can look back. I did a bit of bird and I think it was when I was going in front of my parole board and they read out my record and I shivered and thought, Well, I'll never get parole. Then they read the new report and I thought I wasn't a nice person at all, not at all. I had thought I was a nice person, but I wasn't. That changed me, but I think I've still got to do a little bit of learning now.

LIFE OF CRIME

The skulduggery started when I was sixteen. A lot of it was to do with the institutions I was in. My sister is mentally handicapped – she couldn't get out. But I could; I got out with my mates and I thought, Well, if they're up to skulduggery, then I'm up to skulduggery, too. You wouldn't believe the amount of times I got nicked and allowed myself to be carried home!

Since then I've done enough bird to know I don't want to go inside again. It was never violence as such – I'm a disciplined martial artist. I was done for allowing myself to be carrying offensive weapons.

IS PRISON A DETERRENT?

If you're the norm – yes. If you're a person with a bit of life, ambition and substance – yes, it is. But if you're not, no, it isn't.

There are loads of people who get up in the morning, whack something up the nose, drink down the pub twenty-four hours a day, go and nick this or that – for them, no. If you've got some substance in your life, you feel prison. If you haven't got a home you're not too bothered where you sleep, are you? I've got substance in my life now. If I'm in prison, I miss my kid, I miss being at home, I miss being with my mates down the pub.

I think the facilities in prison for the disabled are terrible now – I did my bird quite easy – but you wouldn't now. The prison service can't cope with disabled people.

DO YOU BELIEVE IN CAPITAL PUNISHMENT?

Yes, definitely, I do. People who sexually assault and hurt kids. Don't torture them – I'm not into the torture game, that makes us as bad as them. But, certainly, string them up. I honestly believe that if these people knew they would be killed if they hurt or sexually assaulted a child, if they knew they'd be strung up, they wouldn't do it.

WHAT WOULD HAVE DETERRED YOU FROM A LIFE OF CRIME?

Having a proper job. Being respected in the community. It didn't work out like that. If you pick a fight with me, you deserve to get beaten up because you're the kind of person who would take five pounds off my mum in the street.

HAVE YOU EVER BEEN STABBED/SHOT?
I've never been shot, but I've been stabbed in the hand.

SCARIEST MOMENT?
I was once on a boat with my family in the Caribbean. It was three in the morning and I had a nightmare. I suddenly woke up and for some reason I thought my mum was dead. I woke everyone else up and said, 'Get up, up, we're going back to Britain now. NOW!' It was a strange gut feeling, really strong, very scary.

SADDEST MOMENT?
Losing my child, my baby. He was five months old and called DJ – Duch Junior. That day was the worst of my life. The pain was so bad it was physical.

WHAT RATTLES YOUR CAGE?
I can't abide stupidness – stupid rules – don't do this, don't do that ...

HAVE YOU EVER REALLY LOVED ANYONE?
Leave it out – why do you think I'm on my Jack Jones? I could never love anyone else. Can't imagine myself shacked up with any other woman, not the sort of man I am. Love and hate are so close together – if that was love, why do I feel like this now?

I feel so full of hate and bitterness. So how can I say I love? Love is love; love means loving someone endlessly, no matter what they do.

WHAT FRIGHTENS YOU?
My father was a vicar. He's now retired. Only him.

DESCRIBE A HARD BASTARD
Someone who can take it, take it, take it!

NAME A HARD BASTARD
My mum.

WHERE DO YOU SEE YOURSELF IN FIVE YEARS?
Sitting on a yacht in Miami, listening to music and contemplating my next film deal!

ANY REGRETS?
Not really – you come in with nothing, you go out with nothing. Well, maybe, I should have listened to my elders when I was young. Then, perhaps, I wouldn't have had such a hard time growing up.

Dominic

The Milky Bar Kid is strong and tough ... and only the best is good enough. Yep ... that just about sums up Dominic.

Dominic is a big, strong man even if his nickname is The Milky Bar Kid. He's no nerdy geek with glasses. Dominic is a boxer, a heavyweight, a no-messing weight, a knock-out weight.

Normally, I wouldn't include a boxer in my book, although they are all tough guys and disciplined. Boxing is a sport. Mind you, I think boxing and skulduggery have always gone hand in hand to a certain extent ... in certain circles. Many of the villains I've known or been involved with have been involved with boxing to some degree. It's a way of releasing aggression, and many villains are aggressive. To be honest, many of them love a tear-up and better in the ring than in the street. And if you're going to box, then you want to do it well.

Dominic does it well ... he is a hard bastard.

BACKGROUND

I was born in Bethnal Green. I was brought up in Essex, like in Woodford. It was just a normal upbringing, you know what I mean; we didn't have much, but it was normal. I can't say it was bad – I've got a brother and we had our mum and dad who looked after us.

I suppose I was a bit of an animal from the beginning – I mean, I got expelled from junior school. But once I went to senior school it was different. I was a little fish in a big pond then. I left school at fifteen, worked as a car-sprayer, got good money, really good money, then I got fed up with working. So I started doing the doors at eighteen and then I worked all over the place. I worked at The Astoria, The Venue, Dingwalls... The thing was, even at eighteen, I was always game. Even though I had curly hair and glasses – they used to call me The Milky Bar Kid – I was always game. I wouldn't take shit off anyone. I worked with a gang of lorry drivers and once they saw me in a pair of shorts and they said, 'Look, it's Milky!' I didn't have bandy legs but I was very white and the name stuck. But it's actually served me well – it's a comical name people remember. It's done well for me in boxing, too, because kids coming into the game now all like to call themselves Killer or Terminator. I laugh my head off when I'm fighting because they hear that comical name but I'm a born fighter; fighters aren't made, they're born. I think I've wanted to fight since I was born.

I suppose I started seriously when I was twenty or twenty-one, but I was always rucking before that. I was involved in street-fighting before that but, basically, I'm a boxer – and a very good boxer at that. If I could combine everything I've got and if I could listen to my trainer – and he's known me for twelve years now – he says if I can just listen, I'll beat anyone. I enjoy fighting – I always have and always will.

IS PRISON A DETERRENT?

Yes and no, I suppose. You go inside these days and you come out with more knowledge and more connections than you ever had before. Then again, some people go in and come out different people than they ever were before. I do think that going into prison kills your soul – I'd never want to go away if I could help it. I've always wanted to be a free bird.

The life I've got at the moment is very good – I work hard. Don't get me wrong, there's the boxing, but the other work I do, like the debt-collecting, is a hard game because you're always walking in everyone else's shit. It isn't like saying to someone, 'Give me the fucking money' – it's hard. Like me and this other fella, we went to this big Turkish drinking den and there's only us two there and there must have been twenty geezers there – I don't carry anything with me because I don't need anything.

Once inside, they took us to the cellar and we talked and they're all there with cues and everything, and you think you just don't need the aggro, but you've got to do it anyway. Without going into too much detail, we walked out with the dough.

But there really are days when you wake up and think, I don't want to go to work today. I really don't want to do that today. But you've got to – that's where you get your money. We're not horrible people. We'd much rather sit down and work it out.

We're doing a debt at the moment – an old fella – you can't get blood out of a stone. But he still owes money. It's very frustrating, but first you talk. You know when someone's having you on and when someone's telling the truth. It's easy – they owe the money, we want it back.

Sometimes, it's not only the money, it's the principle that matters. We have a 98 per cent success rate – we haven't had to touch anyone really.

DO YOU BELIEVE IN CAPITAL PUNISHMENT?

For nonces, yes, definitely. If I had kids and someone hurt them, I'd hunt them down and I'd do bird for it. Someone fucks about with your kids, you'd do them, wouldn't you? You wouldn't even think about it.

WHAT DETERRED YOU FROM A LIFE OF CRIME?

Looking at other people – and what's happened to them as a result.

HAVE YOU EVER BEEN STABBED/SHOT?

I got a little nick once – that was the first night I worked at the Astoria. I've been threatened a few times but I think if they threaten you, they aren't going to do it. But the life we lead, you've got to expect it, haven't you?

SCARIEST MOMENT?

Upsetting my mum, I think. My mum's an outlaw – I'd rather fight Tyson any day!

SADDEST MOMENT?

Women make for the saddest moments. Most men say they're as hard as nails, but when it comes to women, I wear my heart on my sleeve which, I suppose, makes me the person I am but it also means I've been hurt by women.

WHAT RATTLES YOUR CAGE?

Rudeness. I do like manners in people. If you're on the door and people don't say, 'Thank you', that gives me the fucking hump, that does. If you open the door for someone these days, you try and be nice to them, you say, 'Hello' and 'How are you?' and they think you're mad! All I want is to be happy – I suppose I am a happy-go-lucky person. You expect a thank-you. When you don't get one, that aggravates me.

HAVE YOU EVER REALLY LOVED ANYONE?

Yes. I loved and she done me like a kipper – and that really hurt. So for the last four years or so it's been hard for people to employ me because they know I'll take it as far as it can go. Why not? I'm on my own, I'm a single man. I have nothing to lose.

WHAT FRIGHTENS YOU?

Spiders.

DESCRIBE A HARD BASTARD

Someone who is willing to stand up for what he believes in. Some people out there are physically hard but not mentally – as soon as you get into their nuts, they're in trouble. A hard bastard will do anything for what he believes in – his family, his friends. My loyalty is to my friends; I'd do anything for my friends and they know that.

NAME A HARD BASTARD

One Mr Dark. I don't hero-worship him but he's as close to family as I'm going to get and the toughest man I've ever met.

WHERE DO YOU SEE YOURSELF IN FIVE YEARS?

Hopefully not in prison – hopefully settled with a wife and kids, people I can trust. Because there's one thing I know – there're too many dogs out there. There seems to be so little trust out there nowadays.

ANY REGRETS?

No. Whatever I've done I'd stand up for every day of the week. Some things I've done wrong and I think, I've been a bit lucky there. But then, the important things, the ones that matter, if I've done wrong I've always held my hands up to it. So no regrets.

Manchester
Tony

Manchester Tony loves his dogs, his British bulldogs. And you know what they say about owners growing to look like their dogs – or is it vice versa? I'm sorry, Tony, but you do look strikingly similar and I mean that in the nicest possible way!

I drove to a new housing estate in the depths of the Garden of England – Kent – to meet Manchester Tony. I know – odd! A brand-new Merc was parked in the drive. I sat on his plush leather sofa. Tony handed me a drink in a crystal flute while he shooed his beloved dogs out for a wee.

He was wearing a dark-blue suit which looked like Armani (although I was too embarrassed to ask), grinned a huge grin and rubbed his hands. 'Well, whatya want to know?'

He told me about his Army days ... and about his dogs. He told me about his time inside ... and his dogs.

He told me about Manchester ... and his dogs. I didn't mind. I'm a dog lover, too. So I told him about my two dogs ... and my parrot.

Then we got on to the subject of door work – and fighting. Gone was the beaming smile and the niceties. Out the window with the fluted crystal and even his beloved dogs were given a quick shufty up the bollocks, and the kitchen door slammed behind them.

Tony came alive and I saw the real Manchester Tony. Now it was my turn to grin and rub my hands, now we were talking ...

BACKGROUND

I'm originally from Manchester – obviously – but I came down to London when I was in the Army. I wasn't in for long – went in at sixteen, came out at eighteen. I ended up marrying a girl down here in Woolwich so I stayed. I didn't want to go back to Manchester – there was a bit of a family situation; they didn't like me up there. Manchester is much more segregated than London; people keep to their own areas – it's all to do with race. I joined the Army because, basically, I didn't want to go to school. The training I loved, the discipline I didn't. But since my Army days, I have kept up with the training – I've bought my own gym!

LIFE OF CRIME

My first and only time in prison was because of drugs. But it was only a little bird, nothing much to talk about. I spent some time reading books. Believe it or not, I read yours!

DO YOU THINK PRISON IS A DETERRENT?

No. No way, because I walked into prison and it was like walking down the Old Kent Road, it was like being out on the street again. The only difference was there wasn't women there. Prison was great ... well, great-ish. The only thing I hated was missing the kids, because I wouldn't have them visit me. It's not right.

DO YOU BELIEVE IN CAPITAL PUNISHMENT?

Yes and no. The usual thing – for perverts, rapists, child molesters – yes. They're simply scum.

WHAT WOULD HAVE DETERRED YOU FROM A LIFE OF CRIME?

Having lots of money – that's the only thing, money. I was a bad boy at one point, a total arsehole. When I went to prison, I called my mother to tell her where I was and her answer was, 'Well, it took them thirty-six years to get you there but they got you there in the end.' She always thought I'd end up in prison and she was right. It doesn't matter who you are or how big or clever you think you are, the Old Bill will get you in the end. They always do.

HAVE YOU EVER BEEN STABBED/SHOT?

I've been stabbed once. And I've been shot at a couple of times but they missed – thank God! Both times I was working the door – once was in the club itself.

But when I was stabbed I didn't think, Oh, I won't do this any more – it didn't hurt. I didn't feel it at all when it happened. You don't feel it at the time – you feel it after. I think it's all to do with adrenalin. That red mist comes up and you don't see anything and you don't feel anything. You're in a fight – you just go for it. The red mist doesn't come up as much as it did – I'm more controlled now.

SCARIEST MOMENT?

It's hard to think of one. My scariest moment was working the door and I was tooled up. We bashed this geezer up and just tipped him down the stairs. The meat wagon's pulled up, the Old Bill's come running in. I've got a 3.57 Magnum stuffed down the back of my trousers. They came running in and said, 'You're nicked,' and I just said, 'Oh, bollocks!'

Lucky for me, a friend saw what happened; she took the gun off me and slid out a back door. That was the worst moment of my life. I didn't want to go away for having a gun and not using it – that would be a mug-off.

SADDEST MOMENT?

Missing my kids when I was in prison.

WHAT RATTLES YOUR CAGE?
Liars. I can't stand people who lie. I hate them.

HAVE YOU EVER REALLY LOVED ANYONE?
Yes. My kids. My wife. And my dogs. Not necessarily in that order – whichever way you want to take it. I have to watch what I say here!

WHAT FRIGHTENS YOU?
Losing my dogs. When I lost one of my British bulldogs it broke my heart. I had to have him put down because he was ill – then six weeks later the other one died. I was OK with the first one, but when it happened to the second one, too, it killed me, it really crucified me.

DESCRIBE A HARD BASTARD
A hard bastard isn't a bully-boy. I work on the door and I'm not a bully. I'm nice, I have style and I'm happy until they upset me and then I'll bash them. All these bully-boys around – they're not hard bastards. A hard man is a true man, I think.

NAME A HARD BASTARD
Phil Mitchell – only kidding!

I thought Lenny [McLean] was a hard bastard. I liked Lenny – I met him a few times and he was all right.

WHERE DO YOU SEE YOURSELF IN FIVE YEARS?

Hopefully rich, well-off, comfortable – I'll probably still be on the door. Still be in the gyms. It's all a game, but it's brilliant – it earns respect as well. You get a lot of respect, especially if you're on the right sort of door. Young blokes on the door are all so keen to bash everyone up, but really you don't need to be like that.

That's not my idea of things at all. My only reason to go to work is to earn some money, have a nice night and enjoy myself if at all possible. At the moment, I'm trying to break into something new – to do bodyguarding. I'm looking forward to that. To be honest, I don't have to work the doors any more – financially, I mean. I tried giving it up but I was bored. To be truthful, I like the buzz.

I got into door work unintentionally, like most people do. The first place I worked was Bermondsey, just south of the river in London. I cracked me knuckles every weekend! It was rough. That was my first experience with a shooter – someone stuck a gun up my nostril!

These Bermondsey lads came down to the club and said, 'Let's shoot the doorman!' They came out with a .38. So I've got this gun to my head and the other doormen are at the top of the stairs and I thought, If they come down, I'm dead. For fuck's sake, don't come down those stairs. That was one occasion, another I was standing in the Old Kent Road, when suddenly a red Ford Escort turns up and they shoot and I hit the ground very hard.

That's life on the door. You need to know who's who and what's what. I didn't when I first came to London. But I do now.

ANY REGRETS?
No. None at all. Whatever's happened has all been part and parcel of life.

Conclusion

All these men are from different walks of life; they are different in many ways but so alike in many others. A good percentage – in fact 40 per cent – of the men are not criminals, they are straight guys. Just because they are straight does not mean they're not tough. Many spoke of the 'red mist', an uncontrollable rush of adrenalin and anger so intense that it left them breathless with rage. While experiencing the 'red mist' most felt they were capable of almost anything.

Seventy per cent of the men have, at one time, been stabbed. Each and every one agrees that, incredibly, they never felt the actual stabbing. But afterwards, in the cold light of day, it hurt like hell, especially when the knife was pulled out. Ouch! Ninety-five per cent of the men that had experienced prison agreed that it was a college where they learnt more inside than out.

A better education and having money would be their biggest deterrent from a life of crime – not going to jail.

But what else did they have in common? Undoubtedly they all have an inbred sense of pride and honour. They would rather kill or be killed than let anyone take a liberty with them, that's for sure. Not one of the men I interviewed tried to make excuses for the things they had done, but neither did they apologise. While researching for this book I met lots of 'retired' gangsters, villains, hoodlums and tough guys, all of them reformed characters. Nod, nod, wink, wink – know what I mean?

I'm not going to stand in judgement of these men. It was not my job to criticise them or challenge them on what they were telling me. That was not my intention. I knew just what they were capable of or I wouldn't have been interviewing them. I was questioning them as a journalist. I'm just reporting the facts like a war correspondent – yeah, that's it, a war correspondent. Because it is a war and, at times, while interviewing – or interrogating them, as some of the men claimed I was doing – it felt like I was in the middle of a bleedin' war zone.

Cor, mate, these men can be paranoid and touchy! If any of them got wind of who I was interviewing for the book they would sneer, 'He's a tosser! What you talking to him for?' Or 'I'd do 'im any day.' It was like treading in a minefield. So I never mentioned who was in my book. I became sneaky, and lied. Yes, I admit it, I lied mercilessly and I don't care. It's my feckin' book and I put in who I feckin' well like! Oh dear, I just saw a bit of the red mist. I think I've been hanging around these tough guys too long ...

But, seriously, I didn't intend to get dragged into the politics of who's who and what's what. The only thing that mattered was this: is the geezer a tough guy? If the answer was yes, I included them. If the answer was no, I left him out. Plain and simple.

All the men in this book are as tough as nails. Hardcore – they know the score! I've heard it said that some of the men are tough on the outside and soft in the middle. Well, I suggest that you bite one and see...